To Mary

a book about my
life as a young boy.

All the Best!

Tom Klobuchar

The
TAILOR'S
SON

A Story of Forgiveness and
God's Amazing Grace

The TAILOR'S SON

A Young Man's Journey to Find
the Fatherhood of God

THOMAS S. KLOBUCHER

The Tailor's Son
A Young Man's Journey to Find the Fatherhood of God

© 2014 All Rights Reserved, Thomas S. Klobucher.

Published by

NEXTIS PRESS
476 Brighton Drive
Bloomingdale, Illinois 60108 USA
www.thetailorsson.com

Cover and Interior Design: AuthorSupport.com
Cover Imagery: Shutterstock
Author Photography: Michael Hudson Photography

978-0-9848469-6-2 (Hardback)
978-0-9848469-7-9 (Paperback)
978-0-9848469-8-6 (Ebook)

Printed in the United States of America

DEDICATION

This book is dedicated to the memory of my father, John Klobucher, who told me the best stories of my childhood. He also challenged me to dream big dreams and taught me about the joy of good work. And it is dedicated to the memory of my dear mother, Rose Klobucher, who made each one of her five children think that she loved that one the most. Words cannot express my gratitude for her earnest prayers and loving advice to me, her wayward son, while I was in my early teens

TABLE OF CONTENTS

ACKNOWLEDGMENTS

First and always, I want to give thanks to God the Father, who offers to us all the Fatherhood of God—the opportunity to be adopted into his forever family, if we will put our faith and trust in Him alone.

My deep gratitude goes out to my father and my mother, John and Rose Klobucher; my wife Carol, who is my soul mate, my partner, my best friend and encourager, and the one person who always makes me want to be a better man; and my two children, Lisa and Paul, their spouses, Mark and Amy, and their five children, Kate, Jenna, Seth, Caden, and Kelsy.

I'm especially grateful to God for the memory of my oldest sister, Rose K. Kammerling, who saved my life and guided me as a young man to do the right thing, and who was always there for me in times of need. She was a solid rock of strength.

Thanks go out to all of the associates at our firm, Thomas Interior Systems, who made it a truly Great Place to Work.

And I also want to thank Brandon Toropov of iWordSmith, my editor and friend, who guided me and inspired me to stay the course; to Victoria Wright of Bookmark Services, who did the final rounds of editing and cheered me on across the finish line; to Jerry Dorris of AuthorSupport.com for the cover design and layout of the book interior, along with much advice along the way; to my longtime friend Ed Hoover, who was the first person to tell me that I needed to write books; and to Pastor Mark Bubeck, Pastor Ray Pritchard, Dave Patty, Josh Patty, Dann Spader, and all the others who offered support, advice, and encouragement along the way.

Special thanks go to you, the reader, for investing your time and attention in this book. My hope is that you will be blessed by it, and that you will share it with others who have not yet experienced the Fatherhood of God.

FOREWORD

Who can explain what it means to be your father's son?

Most men spend a lifetime trying to figure that out, and once we do, our father is often already gone.

Fathers give us our last name and our heritage, and they teach us things that lie so deep that we don't even know that we know them. Many years ago when our oldest son, Josh, was just a little boy, a friend said they saw us walking side by side down the street. I had my right hand in my pocket and my left hand was swinging by my side. Josh walked next to me, with his right hand in his pocket and his left hand swinging by his side.

Just a few days ago my wife and I were sitting next to Josh and his three-year-old son, Knox, when she pointed to Knox and then to Josh. I looked and there they were, father and son, slightly leaning forward, both of them tapping their left foot at the same time.

No one had to tell Josh to be like me.

No one had to tell Knox to be like Josh.

And so it goes, from fathers to sons in every generation.

A big part of life for any young man comes in the hard task of discovering who he really is. Danish philosopher Soren Kierkegaard said it this way, "And now, with God's help, I will become myself."

We need God's help to discover who we really are. As Tom Klobucher points out in vivid terms, his own voyage of self-discovery required God's help in some very difficult moments. In this remarkably candid book, Tom tells us about a father whom he admired, who set a high standard of hard work, who came to this country as an immigrant, and in true American fashion, started with nothing and made something of himself.

Along the way he and Tom had a falling out. Tom would say that was mostly his own fault. It is certainly not unusual.

Most men can look back on strained moments with their fathers, even with men whom they admired and desperately wanted to please. Perhaps that admiration makes the strain inevitable.

But along the way and to his own great surprise, Tom found the Lord. He discovered a Heavenly Father who loved him completely and who made the ultimate sacrifice in the death of his Son, Jesus Christ. Tom found a God who loved him and pursued him and brought him into his Forever Family. In the end, Tom and his father became eternally connected as the Lord Jesus brought them back together again.

As you read *The Tailor's Son*, you will meet a father and son whose story is unique and yet universal. And you will have an opportunity to get to know your Heavenly Father in a very personal way.

Every son needs to know his earthly father.

Every son needs to know his Heavenly Father.

Stay tuned. This story has the power to grab your heart. If you are ready, it could also change your life.

Ray Pritchard, President

Keep Believing Ministries

Author: *An Anchor for the Soul, Man of Honor, The ABCs of Wisdom*

Editor's Comments

It was an honor to hear Tom's story, and an even deeper honor to help to edit it. This book brought me closer, not just to him as a friend, but to the American experience itself.

Tom's story begins in the early years of the past century, when things like the long ocean voyage, the lonely experience of the European immigrant, and the trials and opportunities of Ellis Island were not pieces of distant history, but powerful present-tense realities. His story ends in a timeless moment, the moment of reconciliation of two long-estranged human hearts: the heart of a son and the heart of a father. In between there is a test of faith and a personal rededication to that faith, another deeply American theme.

Having known Tom for some years, and having worked with him on several books, I had caught glimpses of his relationship with his father in little snippets, here and there. I thought it was the story of an entrepreneur, but I was wrong. It is the story of America.

– Brandon Yusuf Toropov

PROLOGUE

Like Father, Like Son

A s I sit here in my home office looking at the family pictures on my bookshelves and on the walls, I see my father and my mother, along with my four siblings. I see my wife Carol and our children, both when young and grown up. I see my children's children—my grandchildren—all of them looking down at me as if to say, "Dad, we are counting on you."

From the shelf, I pick up one of my father's antique pipes and smell the sweet, rich aroma from the tobacco that was baked into the briarwood bowl perhaps forty or fifty years ago; pipe smoking was one of Dad's great loves. As I hold it, the memory of my father calls out to me. It says, "Be the man I taught you to be."

Then I look back to the photos on the wall. I can almost hear my dad saying, "Tom, be the man we need you to be." He has been gone for thirty years now, but he is not forgotten.

It's not easy, this business of being a father, a son, a husband. And it's certainly not easy trying to write about it. I reached a point in my life when I realized it was time to do just that: to write down my experiences for all of them, and perhaps for you. What follows is my own attempt to describe some of the father and son events that I have experienced and learned from, as well as how these events, along with heredity, shape who we become. After all, we are our fathers' sons. Along the way, perhaps I can help others, too. Perhaps this book will resonate with you as well.

My dad always tried to do the right thing, to be a good example for those who followed. And that's what I'm doing here: striving to do the right thing. It's a difficult journey. I am steadied by the thought that I'm not making this journey alone. That my father and his father, that my children and grandchildren, and mighty God the Father, are all walking with me.

Even now, the smell of my father's pipe takes me back to my childhood years.

PART ONE

The Great Journey

1948

This Story Begins in the late summer of 1948, with a young boy pressing his nose firmly against the plate glass storefront window of a tailor's shop in LaSalle, Illinois.

Back then, a coke and burger cost less than fifty cents. Harry Truman was the president. And most people still went out and got measured for at least one suit of clothes. It was a major status symbol—everyone who was anyone had one. That meant most towns had at least one tailor's shop, and the tailor and the customers always seemed to be on display. In this case, it was my dad (the tailor) and the president of the local bank (the customer, getting fitted for a new suit of clothes).

That little boy was me, that shop was my dad's, and if 1948 seems like along time ago to you, you can rest assured that it seems like several lifetimes ago to me. I was actually a whole different person who watched through that window so carefully as his father measured up another local businessman for another new suit of clothes. I look back now through the years at that young boy, and at the dad he stood in awe of, with a sense of amazement. How long the journey to come. How different the journey of each of the two travelers before their arrival at their destination.

A JOURNEY THROUGH TIME

Making that journey through time is not always easy, and none of us can get out of it. We each are given a certain amount of time to pass through. Either we do it well, or we do it poorly. This book is about that journey, the job of becoming the person you were really meant to become, and it is also about the role that fathers have to play in that journey, particularly for young men who feel they may have been left behind.

I wrote this book because I was inspired by certain beliefs I picked up along the way during my own journey.

I believe that God the Father stands by every family and every child.

I believe that angels wait to guide us...if only we are willing to follow them.

I believe that God is always waiting to help in the fathering process.

FAMILY MATTERS

Of course, every family is different. And every human father is unique.

Some fathers are really good at what they do: they get it. They know how to be there for their children. They themselves may not have been fathered well. Perhaps they were not fathered, in any emotional sense, at all. They may have had experiences in their own lives that made their own growing-up process easy or difficult. Yet these fathers wish to be there for their children. They want to get it right.

God bless these men. Many of them, I know, didn't have the best upbringings, but they made the best of the situation and stepped up so they could become great fathers to the young people in their lives.

For the rest of us, the current statistics are working against us. Experts tell us that two out of three marriages end in divorce. There is a deficit in our culture when it comes to fathering. Many children are left more or less fatherless, and this leads to varying degrees of dysfunction. The fathers who disappear have no great role in their children's lives. They are not bad men; usually, they just don't know how to do the difficult job that has been put in front of them, especially in the case of a divorce.

THE OPEN QUESTION

No child has a choice when it comes to determining what kind of human father he or she will have, or whether there will be a human father figure at all. This means some adjustment is necessary...and the question of whether that will be a good adjustment or a slide into darkness is always an open one.

This book is about a good father and his son, in happy times of learning and hard times of dysfunction. I wrote the book remembering both kinds of times, and remembering the days when my own question seemed to be an open one.

The story starts well and ends well, with a very difficult middle for both the father and the son. It is a story of transformation made possible by the Father of us all.

WELCOME TO MY WORLD

In the late summer of 1948, a lot of businesses were still recovering from the hardships of the past war. Many small businesses in LaSalle, Illinois, had closed, but I noticed that there always seemed to be someone in my dad's shop getting measured up for a suit. The fact was that if you had a job or you wanted a job, or if you anticipated getting married or buried someday, you needed a suit. At least, that's what my dad always told me.

My dad, John Klobucher, was both a gifted tailor and a master of promotion and public relations. He marketed his business in a way that didn't rely on paid advertisements, brochures, or anything else like that. He had a powerful way of advertising the latest new designs for menswear, but it didn't involve buying space in local newspaper. He took a more personal approach. My dad was a walking billboard.

THE CIGAR WALK

Twice a day, once in the late morning and once in the late afternoon as people were getting out of work, Dad would embark on what we all called his "cigar walk." It always lasted at least a mile. He wore a great suit, sported a classy fedora, and puffed a big cigar as he wound his way through the heart of the LaSalle business district. Whatever route he chose, he always went past the banks; past City Hall; past the two clandestine gambling halls it seemed that every male in town knew about (I recall they were fronted by a barbershop and a cigar store, respectively); past all the popular bars where the businessmen would stop for a drink. My dad was no drinker, but he knew how to make an impression in those watering holes—and everywhere else where businessmen could be found. Anywhere prospects were, that just happened to be someplace he wandered on his cigar walk.

There were two cigar walks every weekday; that was a rule my dad held to without exception. Every time he took one of these walks, he was dressed impeccably in his own finely tailored suits, which he himself had tailored. He always presented himself in the latest fashion, and he always looked great. He always puffed that huge cigar as he strolled. It was as a simple action that drew a lot of attention to him. That cigar garnered more attention than a printed advertisement would have, I think.

The cigar walks established my dad as the best (and only!) tailor in town. He made quite an impression on these walks, and it was always great. He was committed to leaving that great impression twice a day. The outfit he wore in the morning was always different from the one that he wore that afternoon.

My dad, John Klobucher, was a walking advertisement for his business, Klobucher's Klothes Shop. To this day, I can't imagine a more effective marketing campaign for that business.

WHERE THE ACTION WAS

My family lived behind the shop, but the real action, I always sensed, was up front where my dad worked.

In those early days of my life, I spent many hours watching through the front window or—if my dad waved me away, which he sometimes did—hidden deep in the clothes racks in the shop, watching my father work. When I was inside the shop, I could listen to him, too, as he fitted the customer with just the right tailored fit for a new suit of clothes. Somehow, I always thought that my dad knew that I was there, hiding in the clothes rack and listening. In fact, once in a while he would actually pause, turn toward the rack, and wink his eye. There was always a lot of discussion that went into measuring someone for a good suit of clothes. I remember the smell of the shop: cigars and steam-irons pressing the wool meant for men to wear.

There was a sitting area and a showroom area. Both of those spaces positively overwhelmed you with the smell of wool under that steam-iron presser. It's a smell I still strongly associate with my father and his tailor shop. When I smell any of those things now, it's 1948 again, and I am back in that shop, watching him work.

I remember there were wool sample swatches everywhere. Once you made it into the showroom area, you encountered racks and racks of men's suiting materials, mostly wool hanging on display against the walls. On one wall near the shop door was a sign bearing dad's favorite saying: "Too soon we get old...too late we get smart."

The clean smell of the wool, and the sight of that newly woven material neatly arrayed, conveyed the sense of being able to start all over again—that shop left you feeling that you could be, do, or become anything you wanted in life. With the right suit, the right material, the right styling, you could leave the same kind of powerful impression that a movie star, or a top business executive, or my dad, might leave.

THE QUESTIONS

There was a very powerful visual and sensory message on display in that shop, and it always took the form of a question: Who do you want to be? What do you want to accomplish? What is your best vision of yourself now and in your future?

My dad used that showroom to ask those questions in countless ways, during interactions with countless prospects. Somehow, though, he and I never really settled on the best answers to those questions in my own case. I still don't know why that was. All I can tell you is, we never quite figured it out.

I remember the sight of racks and racks of suits being finished or altered. And always, always, the sound of my dad asking his customers questions. What work did they do? What kind of job where they interviewing for? How had they decided on that? What did they see themselves doing four or five years down the line? It put his customers at ease, and it helped him to do a better job. He never cut a suit of clothes for someone unless he understood that person's aspirations in life. Dad's suits were never made for the man standing before him, but for the man he aspired to become.

That left an enduring impression on people. And when I say enduring, I mean enduring. Recently, in my research for this book, I spoke with a Chicago-area banking executive who informed me that, over a fifty-five-year period, four generations of her family had started their professional careers by buying suits from my father's store!

What I was watching when I eavesdropped on my father's discussions with his customers was about tailoring clothes, but it was also about tailoring something else: a person's self-image. To create the right suit for the customer, my father had to measure more than dimensions of the customer's figure. He had to take the measure of the man.

I didn't know it at the time, but as I listened to my father and his discussions with customers, I was learning the basics of selling, listening, customer service, envisioning. All of that served me well through my later career in business.

But looking back, I don't recall my dad actually asking me those questions.

BUMPS IN THE ROAD

It would be nice to be able to tell you that everything that passed between my dad and me after that moment in late August 1948 was serene and harmonious. But it wouldn't be true. There were bumps in the road.

When I was seven years old, I thought he could do no wrong, but as we moved onward through the years and I passed into youth and adulthood, the dynamic between us changed. I know that stories in which fathers and sons have few problems with each other are rare, and when they do show up, they tend to make for pretty dull reading. The story of how my father and I made it through my young teen years, for better or for worse, is not a dull one.

My father and I had a big falling out in the years that followed, and we did not reconcile until some years later. Fortunately, while we still had time together, I was able to tell him how much he had meant to me and how much I had learned from him. And by the way, I know that conversation was a gift to both of us from God the Father.

Make no mistake. This book is about that Father, too—God, the Father of us all. He is the one who is the beginning and the end, and always has our best interests in mind, no matter how life seems to be unfolding for us at the time.

PART TWO

Portrait Of A Plugger As A Young Man

THE EARLY LOVE, THE LATE LOVE, AND WHAT CAME IN BETWEEN

God the Father saw to it that I grew up the son of a tailor. This tailor was a strict disciplinarian, a hard worker, and a good provider, a man from the "old country" whom I idolized—at least, I did back then, as a youngster growing up and figuring everything out for the first time.

I came to love him that deeply again, too. In between, there was a lot of drama, as there is so often between fathers and sons.

I know now that the drama was part of what God had in mind for my father and me, and though it was difficult to go through at the time, I am so grateful for both the hard times and the good times—for all the time I had with him.

This book is here now because I decided that I did not want to let my own time pass without at least trying to write about our life together: the close times, the distant times, the learning times, and the reconciliation that made it all worthwhile. All of it, every step of the journey, helped to make me a better father to my own kids. As you will see, the early teen years in my life were very difficult. Looking back on them now, though, I know that God used them to make me a better man.

But I'm getting ahead of my story.

THE IMMIGRANT

My father, John Klobucher, came to America through Ellis Island in 1913. He was sixteen at the time he made that journey. In those days, the country he came from was called Yugoslavia. Now, we call it Slovenia, a country of about two and a half million people. This little slice of

European land changed hands six times during World War II. I know because my father followed the news from Europe very closely during the war, and he talked often about the trials of his homeland. He called Slovenia the "sunny side of the Alps."

My father's parents were named Stefan and Barbara. His last name used to be Klobucar, but the fellow checking him in at Ellis Island "Americanized" it.

He spoke no English when he left for America, and he had no idea what the man behind the desk at Ellis Island was doing to his name. Long after he made it through processing, he was able to study his papers closely and figure out what happened. His name became Klobucher.

WHY HE CAME TO AMERICA

My father was the third son in a farming family. As you may know, the oldest son in a European family almost always takes over the family farm, and that's the way my grandfather Stefan ran the family. My father, being a young entrepreneur, saw the handwriting on the wall and began to look for a way to get passage to America, the promised land of milk and honey.

His father, though, was less enthusiastic about the idea. There always was a need for an extra hand to work on the farm. My dad saw this as a green light for him to leave, even though he was only sixteen years old. Somehow he found a way to book passage on a ship to America in 1913. He turned seventeen on the ship.

As it happened, though, the oldest son, George, had other ideas as well, and he also immigrated to America in about 1917 and ended up in a Slovenian community in Cannonsburg, Pennsylvania. He married and found good work and a better life there.

THE SURVIVOR

I was never given a very close-up look at exactly how he managed to make the trip alone, at just seventeen, or what happened to my dad in the first few months after he made it to the United States, but the little information I did get helped me to understand that my dad was, first and foremost, a survivor.

Here was this fresh-faced kid with just a little hard-earned money in his pockets, a dream of a better life, and only a few words of English. He was stepping off the boat and into the heart of New York City at a time when it was more crowded than Calcutta and considerably less friendly to newcomers. The bravery and focus it takes to make that kind of journey, and come out of it with your head screwed on straight and your values in place, is something most people can't imagine these days. I don't know exactly how he made it through that ocean passage, and the even more difficult passage out of Ellis Island, in one piece, but I know that he did.

One thing I also know is that there were plenty of con artists prowling the streets of New York City during that period. Somehow, my dad got taken by one of them. He was a perfect target: literally right off the boat, with no friends or family nearby, and no easy way to get in touch with his relatives in Pennsylvania. Someone who spoke his language approached him, made him feel at home, and took advantage of him. How much the loss amounted to in financial terms, I was never able to figure out—he was reluctant to talk about the details—but I suppose it was substantial. Whatever it was that he lost, I know he gained some important resources in return: a healthy skepticism about the motives of strangers, an instinct for self-preservation, the ability to take a punch, and a capacity to keep his thoughts to himself. There was a Bible verse that my Dad paraphrased frequently while I was growing up. It was the twenty-eighth verse of the seventeenth chapter of Proverbs, and it reads: Even a fool when he holdeth his peace is counted wise: and he that shutteth his lips is esteemed a man of understanding. The way my dad put it though, was: "If you tell everything that you know, then you don't know nothin.'"

That attitude got him past the mean streets of New York and eventually led him to Illinois, where his destiny (and mine) would play out.

WORK AND APPLE PIE

When Dad arrived at Ellis Island, he knew several English words: work and apple pie. While I was growing up I got used to him telling a story about how he made it through those first few days in America. He used to say that he found work right away, but he got very tired of eating apple pie at every meal! That's all he knew how to order at restaurants and rooming houses.

That story became a family tradition of sorts, and to tell you the truth, it got repeated so often that by the time I reached young adulthood, it had kind of faded into the back ground for me. By the time I reached my teens, that story was just a pleasant series of familiar words, something that people said over and over again about my dad or that he said about himself. It was a bookmark of sorts, a placeholder that stood for all that had taken place in his life in that amazing period between the moment he got off the boat and the day he somehow made it through to supporting himself in a country where he literally knew no one, had no allies, and could not communicate in the native tongue. It seemed impossible. But that's what pluggers did: the impossible.

TIGHT QUARTERS

I have to make a comment now about my life with my parents and siblings during my fifteen years at home: Nobody's perfect! I know I wasn't. We were a family of seven people living and learning together in a small three-bedroom, one-bath home behind that tailor shop. It was not always easy. But it was all we knew, and usually, it was just fine.

Some might tend to focus on the negative, on the things that could have been better, on the stuff that we didn't have, on the life that others enjoyed. We were the children of an immigrant father—entrepreneur and business owner—and his devoted wife.

I decided many years ago that I wanted to focus not on the negative, but only on the positive learning experiences that I received from my father, the businessman and entrepreneur, and also from my mother, Rose Ann, the most loving and kind person I have ever met in my life. I have tried to follow that standard in this book. My mom and my dad were doing their very best to raise an all-American family, which was something neither one of them had experienced themselves. They did a good job. They always came back to the principle of hard work.

SOMETHING VERY AMERICAN

Looking back now, and having set out on my own great American journey on the sometimes rocky road of entrepreneurship, I find myself thinking about just how much trial, pain, sacrifice, and hardship that family story about "work and apple pie" covered. I think of how much my dad must have gone through in his life to reach the point where he was even ready to raise a family. I've also thought many times, since I began raising my own family, about the great generosity of spirit necessary to endure what he must have endured in those early days in America, and come out of it, not with bitterness, but with a story about apple pie.

There is something very American indeed about the response to his great transition, something that is important about that period of history, and the nation that grew toward the America we enjoy today, something about work and apple pie that I like to think I have passed on to my own kids and grandkids. At least I have tried.

Refugees and immigrants arriving on America's shores today face a very different reality than the one my father faced, and I know that is probably as it should be. I still feel, though, that we should acknowledge what that earlier generation of immigrants had to overcome in the early years of the previous century. No one offered my dad a free place to stay, or told him how to get health care, or sent him to college paid for by the government, or gave him a cash allowance every month to cover the costs of food and lodging. All of that is waiting for you now, if you come to America under the terms of the present refugee program. In 1913, such protections did not exist. After landing on Ellis Island, you were on your own. That's what my dad was when he arrived in this country—on his own. And I guess it wasn't until I had started a family and launched a company of my own that I realized just how deep the loneliness he must have experienced in his adopted country, and just how hard he must have worked to win that piece of apple pie.

THE PLUGGER

Today, we would use the word entrepreneur to describe guys like my dad, but back in the day, the word was plugger.

This was a guy who hit the road, worked hard, and sold stuff, or made stuff, or worked odd jobs to make ends meet. That's what a plugger did. Pluggers were creative hard workers, and they were endlessly resourceful. If they got knocked down a few times, they always found a way to get back up. They never quit. Some of them decided they had to sell things, so they sold whatever they could, and they sold it well enough to survive, because they knew deep down that they just couldn't quit. Others just found work in another city—farming work, manufacturing work, whatever—by riding the rails in open box cars. My dad did all of that.

Today, we say the word "hobo," and we think of a man without a job who begs for his dinner. We forget that there were a lot of pluggers hitching rides on those trains, a lot of guys following the work wherever it was out there to be found and then working hard once they found it. They'd follow the harvest across the country, checking their suitcases at a hotel for twenty-five cents while they worked somewhere for a week. They didn't sleep in the hotels, though. They slept in the cornfields, haystacks, and barns, and at the end of the week, they would collect their suitcase, which had everything they owned in it, and move on, usually west.

Maybe they would head for steel mills in Gary or copper mines in the upper peninsula of Michigan. They would check their suitcase into the hotel safe for another week or more, and work some more. No welfare. No food stamps. No social security. Just a suitcase, a quarter, and the ability to put in an honest day's work and build up something better for yourself.

My dad was one of those guys. He was a plugger. We forget about those guys now, I guess, but they built big chunks of the country's body, and most of its soul. I think they deserve to be remembered, and they deserve the label they wore with pride long before the word entrepreneur came along: plugger.

GETTING OFF THE RAILS

After a decade or so of riding the rails in open boxcars, my dad finally decided to listen to his elder brother.

That elder brother, named George, was now married and living in Cannonsburg, Pennsylvania. Dad's brother had been dropping hints for years that it might just be time to start thinking about settling down. People got married a lot earlier in those years than they do today, and twenty-seven, in my dad's family at least, was pretty old for a bachelor. This conversation apparently went on for several years, often by mail.

My dad's elder brother told him it might make sense to start consolidating himself and building for the future. In later years, my dad would tell his own kids to know when it was time to "find a job and make it better," and I suspect that this was the kind of advice that my dad got, with increasing urgency, in his letters from my uncle.

Eventually, Dad got a letter that came out and put the cards right on the table. There was a marriageable young woman of Slovenian heritage (my future mother) in the Cannonsburg area who might be interested in discussing matrimony with him. Her name was Rose Ann; she was my uncle's sister-in-law. She was twenty-one years old. Would my dad be interesting in writing to her?

Dad decided to take him up on it.

A six-month correspondence followed, and before too terribly long it was evident to both of them that the correspondence had turned into a courtship. It's hard to imagine someone conducting that kind of longhand courtship now, although I suppose there is probably a social media equivalent these days that involves a compatibility test, shared profile, photographs, and lots of e-mails. None of those options existed all those decades ago for my parents, so for them, the initial encounters all took place in pen-and-ink letters, mailed from Illinois (where my dad was working and saving up money) to Pennsylvania (where my mom lived with her father).

Six months into their correspondence, without ever having seen Rose Anne's face, my dad proposed to her.

"YES—IF"

She accepted...provisionally.

My mom wrote back and told my dad that her answer was yes—if. If he was willing to drive out to Cannonsburg, so they could spend the day together and see how things went when they spent some time together. If they both still agreed that it made sense after they'd been able to have a few conversations, and if my dad was amenable to the idea of them settling down somewhere other than Cannonsburg, Pennsylvania. (That last "if" requires a little explanation, which I'll share with you in just a moment.)

All three of those conditions made sense to my dad. He wrote back and told her so, and he told her when she could expect him to arrive in Cannonsburg for their long-awaited, properly chaperoned day together.

So it was that my dad set out from LaSalle, Illinois in his 1922 Chevy coupe bound for Cannonsburg, Pennsylvania, a distance of 450 miles, to see whether or not it made sense for him to marry Rose Anne.

ALL SMILES

Fortunately for me and my siblings, it did make sense, and the two of them agreed at the end of that big, well-chaperoned day that everything still made perfect sense to both of them. At the end of the day, they were smiling broadly as my dad announced that he would be back in one month to pick up his bride, drive her to Illinois, and start their new life together. With that, he said goodbye to his brother (soon to become his brother-in-law, as well), his brother's wife, Mary, and Rose Anne.

Our family history does not record whether or not he kissed her goodbye after their first meeting, but I like to think he did. What we do know is that at the end of that long day he got right back into his Chevy coupe and began that long, bone-rattling drive back to Illinois.

WHY MOM WANTED TO LEAVE CANNONSBURG

I promised you an explanation for my mom's eagerness to get out of Cannonsburg, and here it is. She and her elder sister, Mary, had years before experienced a very difficult loss: their mother had died when they were both young girls. When Mom's elder sister married my uncle and set up house with him, that more or less left my mom as the woman of the house. That had been quite a challenge for her because, after losing his wife, her dad had begun drinking heavily. This problem had, in large measure, been what motivated her sister to get married to my uncle, a change that left my mom as the "chief cook and bottle washer" in what we would today call a dysfunctional family. At the time when Dad began writing to my mom, she was not only doing the cooking, cleaning, and washing, not only working fulltime in a pottery factory as the sole breadwinner, and not only looking after her father, she was also having a lot of conflicts with her father. Some of those fights apparently got pretty intense. Although I don't remember meeting my grandfather, legend has it he was not an easy man to get along with.

The truth of the matter was that my uncle was solving two problems at once when he stepped forward as matchmaker. The first was a younger brother who hadn't yet settled down, and was getting a little long in the tooth for a bachelor. At that point he was aged thirty. And the second problem was a sister-in-law who was trapped in an unhealthy, unfulfilling and probably unstable home situation with a father who she now found pretty hard to live with.

As my dad drove away in his 1922 Chevy coupe, three people back in Cannonsburg were very happy indeed that everything had worked out between my dad and my mom once they'd finally gotten to spend some time face-to-face: my uncle, his wife, and of course my mom, who was happiest of all. But there was one guy in Cannonsburg who was downright disgusted with the arrangement: my grandfather, who refused to give his blessing to the match. As far as anyone could make out, though, his disapproval didn't make a lot of difference to my mom.

I've told you already that my dad was a plugger, a guy who finds a way to add value, get paid, and get by, no matter what else was happening in the larger economy. There were a lot of pluggers who made it through The Great Depression just fine, and I'm proud to be able to say that my dad was one of them.

I think you can also tell by this point in the book that my dad took the whole institution of marriage pretty seriously, a lot more seriously than a lot of people take it today. Now, we live in a time when people get married after they've had the chance to live together for a while and figure out how to adapt to each other. Then, once they've gotten used to the daily routine of cohabiting, they figure out whether or not they're serious about the relationship. (Or maybe a baby comes along to make them decide whether or not they're serious.) After going through all of that, they might choose, a few years later, to announce to the world that they've made the decision to formalize things and get married.

That's not the way it was in my dad's day. First you decide whether or not you were serious, then you made a commitment, and figured out how to adapt. Pretty much the opposite of what we see now. My dad would have had some strong words about anyone who approached marriage the way many couples do now. Back then, you got serious first, then you got married, then you stuck around and made it work. That was his world.

I tell you all of this so that it will be a little easier for you to understand just how serious my dad was about the idea of marriage…and how much preparation mentally, physically, and financially, he had devoted to the idea of getting serious before he'd even gunned the engine of the '22 Chevy coupe so he could head out and meet my mom face-to-face for the very first time. For the past few years, my dad had been saving up his money, pinching every penny until it bled, in anticipation of being able to ask the right girl to marry him, even though he wasn't quite sure, when he started out, just who that right girl might be.

TWO HOMESTEADS

On that long-awaited day when he and my mom met for the first time to "to see how things went," my hardworking dad owned not one but two properties suitable for raising a family: a property in LaSalle, Illinois, that he planned to eventually build out into a home and storefront where he could open up a tailor shop; and a small "hobby farm" in Manton, Michigan.

Though the farm was not large enough to produce much of an income, it did bring my dad back to his agricultural roots in Europe. These two properties sent a message. He was ready to get serious, and that was part of what he'd come out to Cannonsburg to tell my mom.

29

He wasn't kidding. This was real. He'd been working a long time for this, and he wanted it to work out.

When he finally made his way back to Cannonsburg a month later, my mom and everyone else in her family knew for sure that this union was for real. They all knew that my dad had gotten serious about this. He had come back, because he was committing everything that he had worked for up to this point and everything that might happen to him afterwards, entirely to my mom. Her sister was delighted to see him again, because it meant my mom was moving out of a bad situation. Dad's brother was delighted, too, because it was obvious to him that my dad was doing the right thing, and his wife was happy about what was going on, which I'm sure he didn't mind, either.

My mom was glowing, we are told, on the second day that she got to spend in person with my dad. I guess she knew it was the beginning of a whole new chapter for her. Her father might not have been glowing all that brightly, but that didn't stop her from getting into my dad's Chevy, waving good-bye to all she had known, and starting out to build a whole new life in a growing community called LaSalle, Illinois, which was about ninety miles southwest of Chicago.

A STOP ALONG THE WAY

They had decide to settle in LaSalle, but the drive all the way there was (and still is) quite a long one, so my dad stopped at his property in Manton, which is a few hundred miles away from Cannonsburg. Before they got to the farm, my mom informed him in no uncertain terms that they were going to have to tie the knot legally before they spent the night under the same roof. My dad had been thinking along the same line; he made their first stop in Manton the courthouse, where they found a justice of the peace to do the honors.

They exchanged vows in Manton and were officially husband and wife. No, there hadn't been a big family party to mark their nuptials, but there was a dawning love that they both considered precious, and there were miles and miles of possibility ahead.

They were serious about both of those things.

A WIFE OF NOBLE CHARACTER

I believe their marriage must have been blessed, because it lasted fifty-six years, the rest of my dad's life. I know that my father realized very early on that my mother was to be his helpmate for life. She was the treasure of his life, and he was very lucky to have her.

31

My mother was always helping out in the shop, always finding new ways to support my dad. A Bible verse that I think characterizes the life of my mother—and captures the kind of person she was—is Proverbs 31:10-31. It reads as follows.

Who can find a virtuous woman? Her price is far above rubies. The heart of her husband safely trusts in her, so that he shall have no need of spoil. She will do him good and not evil all the days of her life.

She seeks wool and flax, and works willingly with her hands. She is like the merchants' ships; she brings her food from afar. She rises also while it is yet night and gives meat to her household and a portion to her servant-girls. She considers a field and buys it: with the fruit of her hands she plants a vineyard. She dresses with strength and modesty, and strengthens her arms. She perceives that her merchandise is good: her candle goes not out by night.

She lays her hands to the spindle, and her hands hold the distaff. She stretches out her hand to the poor; yes, she reaches forth her hands to the needy. She is not afraid of the snow for her household: for all her household are clothed with scarlet. She makes herself coverings of tapestry; her clothing is silk and purple. Her husband is known within the city gates, when he sits among the elders of the land.

She makes fine linen and sells it; and delivers garments unto the merchant. Strength and honor are her clothing; and she shall rejoice in time to come. She opens her mouth with wisdom; and in her tongue is the law of kindness. She looks well to the ways of her household and eats not the bread of idleness. Her children arise up and call her blessed; her husband also, and he praises her.

Many women have done virtuously, but you surpass them all. Favor is deceitful, and beauty is vain: but a woman who fears the Lord, she shall be praised. Give her of the fruit of her hands; and let her own works praise her in the city gates.

Part Three

The Falling-Out

A MAN OF FAITH

For most of his life, my dad was not what anyone would call a religious man, but I believe he was always a man of faith. He didn't talk much about what his religious beliefs were, but he knew the difference between right and wrong. He talked about the Golden Rule. He talked about the Ten Commandments. And he could faithfully recite many of the parables of the Bible. I know this because he and I learned them together when I was a boy of eight or nine years.

I remember sitting around the old floor-model Philco radio on Sunday night and listening to the Goodyear Tire and Rubber Company sponsored show, The Greatest Stories Ever Told, which was a very popular radio program back then, one that we both sat and learned from together. Sharing those broadcasts of famous Bible stories with him on Sunday nights—him in his easy chair, me sitting on the floor right in front of him—were some of the most meaningful and important father-and-son times of my life. I can recall him wiping away tears and choking back sobs as we listened to the broadcast. I can recall his hand on my head, ruffling my hair, as the stories issued forth. My dad was not a "I love you" kind of guy; he just didn't have the vocabulary to express emotion in that way as a lot of families do now, but I can tell you that as I listened to those broadcasts with him, I felt loved, and I was happy to be my father's son!

A FATHER'S LOVE

This book is not meant as a comprehensive history of my family, or of my father's life, or even of his relationship with me. Each of those topics could take up a book many times the size of this one. It's a book about the love that can exist between a father and a son, about how our earthly father can be an influence on our direction, on our character, and on what and who we will become in life.

It's also a book about another kind of Father, one whom I also had the opportunity to appeal to at many points during the course of my life. There came a time when my earthly father and I had more distance between us than had seemed possible back when we were listening to that radio show we both loved.

HOPE FOR THE FATHERLESS

Those men who have had a poor father figure in their lives growing up, or had no father at all, may ask, silently or out loud, "What about us? Is there any hope for the fatherless?"

I say the answer is a resounding yes. God in heaven is the Father of us all, and he wants to serve as Father to you and me.

What follows is all about the love that is possible between earthly fathers and sons. It is also about the love our Father God always has waiting for us as we move forward, down the road of our lives—and how that substitute, or adoptive, love of God the Father can stand in the place of the love you might have missed from an absent earthly father.

Looking back now, I realize that any problems I had were my own and not my father's. He was a stern parent, yes, from the European tradition, sterner by far than the parents of any of my friends. But it seems to me that most of my problems centered around my own responses to being a middle son, though at that time of my life I didn't even know what that meant. All of my juvenile temper, all of the misdeeds that got me into heaps of trouble both in and out of school, were just my confused efforts to get noticed by my own family. It seemed to me that I had become the invisible "middle son," who is neither the oldest and most accomplished, nor the youngest and the most in need of protection. The responses I made to that perception of mine were my responsibility, not my dad's or anyone else's.

"GOD SIGHTINGS"

God the Father showed up in my life many times at critical moments when I faced important choices. Each of these God sightings or appearances were at crucial times of my life, when he gave me clear directions and encouragement to make right choices. In the pages that follow, I will share with you how God the Father has truly had his hand upon my life.

You will see that I left home at age fifteen, after having completely squandered my first two years of high school in LaSalle, Illinois. I was a mess. My life was filled with dysfunction, dishonesty, failed grades, alcohol, gang relationships, and police encounters. My father had given up on me and suggested that I drop out of school and get a job at a local factory; my mother was heartbroken. This was a wake-up call

for me. I thought, "This is all that my father thinks I am capable of."
Later on in life, it did occur to me that my father may have used some
great reverse psychology on me with that statement. In essence, he was
saying, "Prove me wrong." If that's what he meant to do, it worked.

I loved my mom, but my father and I had a major disconnect,
and we did not agree on anything at that time. I was truly amazed,
just six years later, when it became clear to me that my father had
somehow become a much wiser man than he had been when he and I
had our falling-out. That's when I finally noticed who and what my
dad really was. My father was a good man, and a great entrepreneur
in his town. In many ways, I realized, our life journeys were quite
similar. They have seemed even more similar to me the further on I
have gone in life. I think I have the "God sightings" to thank for that
recognition, too.

TIMELINE

Even though Dad died almost thirty years ago, he did watch me start
and successfully run my office planning business for seven years before
he died. I know that he was proud of what I did. He told me that he
was proud, and the memory of that still makes me smile even after all
these years.

LIFE TIMELINES FOR MY FATHER AND ME

My Father	Me
Age 13-16	Age 12-15
Disconnected at home	Disconnected at home
Age 16	Age 15
Left home on his own for America and a new life	Left home to live in the Chicago area with older sister and husband
Age 17 to 30	Age 15-36
Worked hard to make his way in a new country. Found work, learned a new language, got a American education and learned the joy of good work.	Worked hard to fit into a new culture in the Chicago area. Made up for lost and wasted time. Fought for a good business education and practical experience. Learned a new positive way of life. Learned the joy of good work.
Age 30	Age 36
Started and ran his own business as an entrepreneur for fifty-plus years.	Started and running my own business as an entrepreneur for thirty-five-plus years and counting.

A part of my father lives on in me and in the lives of my other four siblings. If you have seen me, you have seen my father, however imperfectly, however incompletely, however deeply mixed in with others' influences on my life. But my dad is in there, sure enough, in my face, my voice, my actions, my habits. I even see him in my own children—fainter still, but his influence is there.

My son is like me in many ways. I am like my father in the same ways, and so his influences pass on to the third generation. Sometimes when I visit my relatives, one of them will say, "You remind me so much of your father." There is no finer compliment I could receive. That's what it means to bear my father's name. It is far more than having the same last name.

My dad's character, drive, and personality were in some small way passed on to me. And even though he has been gone for many years, I have a responsibility to preserve his memory, to live up to the things he taught me, to try to be as good a man as he was, and to live in such a way so that people who never knew him will look at me and say," His father must have been a good man." Perhaps, too, the people who did know my dad will read this book and say, "He is a credit to his father's name."

ANOTHER NAME

I am proud to bear my father's name, as you can tell. My dad's last name, though, is not the only name I bear.

I have another name attached to mine, as a Christian; I bear the name of my heavenly Father. Hallowing his name means living in such a way that I increase his reputation in the world. When I've done that well, perhaps people who don't know God will look at my life and say, "He must have had a great God"...and perhaps God will look down from heaven with a smile and say, "That is my son!"

UNFINISHED MEN

Now we reach a question: How do you fill the hole that you have in your heart that was created by what seemed like a missing father, or a poor father figure, or no father at all?

How do you appropriate God the Father as your Best Father?

How do you learn the lessons of fatherhood from the Greatest Father of all, God the Father? And how do you live a satisfying life as a Son of the Father, and be a godly father to your children?

We are all, I think, at least potentially, unfinished men, men in search of the answers to such questions. And I wrote this book to offer my own answers...or, at any rate, the answers that worked for me.

FATHER HUNGER

It is time for a reality check. Perhaps you are one of the millions of men who grew up without a father. Maybe there was a divorce, maybe your father died when you were very young, perhaps your father just walked away, never to be heard from again. Or you have a father, but he is a dysfunctional and poor father figure, and you may be asking, "Is there any hope for me?"

Again, my answer is a resounding yes,yes,yes!

Let me share a story with you that I heard from a missionary leader in Eastern Europe, a story about a young boy who had no father.

There once was a young European boy named Luka who lived in a small village. Luka was an illegitimate child, born out of wedlock and abandoned by his mother, and the father was unknown. Several families in the town cared for him, but for the most part he was alone. By the time he was ten years old, he became the butt of pranks and name-calling. He was mostly called the bastard, which is slang for illegitimate child. Folks would see him in town and yell out, "Hey, Luka, who's your father?"

Luka was a very sad boy who longed to have a father. Life was not good for Luka; he had nowhere else to go. Then one day he heard about a church in town that had a new pastor who was very popular, so Luka started to attend. He would always come late and leave early, so that nobody had time to make fun of him. He liked being in church and really enjoyed listening to the pastor, but he was always the first one out the door, just before the pastor finished talking.

One day, people on both sides of him blocked him into the pew where he was seated, and he could not sneak out in time. He was stuck in the pew, and now the aisles were jammed. He was terrified.

As he edged to the aisle for his escape, he saw a man waiting for him. It was the pastor.

The pastor said in his booming voice, "Hey! I know you. I have seen you here before. Who is your father?"

Luka's heart sank. His mind started to shut down, and the old sadness began to overcome him.

Then the pastor spoke again. "Oh, wait! I know you, I know you...I see your resemblance. You are God's son, and you are here in God's House. You are God's son!

This is your Home. You are always welcome here."

As Luka's eyes began to overflow with tears, the pastor gave him the biggest bear hug that he'd ever received.

Later that day Luka prayed to God the Father and asked him to come into his heart and Luka was adopted into God's forever family, never to feel alone again.

Are you ready to join your forever family?

A FEW THOUGHTS ON MISSING FATHERS

There is a growing body of research on the subject of the missing father figure, on what sons need, on the deep hunger for a father. Focus on the Family recently posted some startling statistics on the subject. Today, well over eight million American households with children under eighteen don't have a father. This leaves the mothers alone, to search for admirable male role models for their sons, or to allow them to grow up without that missing father, and with a hole in their heart where a father should have been. Few, if any of us had the perfect father. There really is only one perfect father. God the Father.

Let me ask you: What does the human father that every son longs for, hungers for, and wished that he had, look like?

Think for a minute about your childhood "guy friends." How many of these acquaintances of yours had a poor father figure or no father at all at home?

I just did a fast census of my grade school class and the neighborhood friends I had when I was a kid. I counted seven boys whom I knew who had no father at home. My list came from the late 1940s into the early 1950s. What would the numbers be today? Much higher, I'm sure.

WHAT A BOY NEEDS FROM A FATHER

Here is an unscientific list of ideal father-to-son characteristics. See how many you might have missed out on...and how many you might be able to share with the son in your life. (Note: An expanded list appears in Appendix B.)

Big heart

Affection, father/son love, camaraderie, protection, strength, learning together, good examples.

Open arms

Acceptance, hanging-out time together, doing guy things, jobs together, garden work, washing the car, ask/answer any question.

Gentle, firm voice

Boundaries, discipline, authority, firm but kind, self-control, calm, not anger, conservative, loving, show love to wife and respect to women and girls.

Happy/fun

Silly fun stuff, wrestling, playing games, contests, playing sports together.

Get dirty fingernails together

Work in the garden, on the lawn, clean up shed or garage

A son seeks to please his father

Encourage and compliment your son. Help him to find ways to please you. Say, "Good job, son! You are the best wheel washer in town!" Compliment him on his work.

Don't be critical and negative

Help him to exercise his gifts, find out what he is good at, and steer him to lots of it.

Coach, teach, show by example

Be a great example to him!

Be a praying Dad

Pray alone and together. Pray for your son and family, as well as with them. Celebrate answered prayers.

We can't be all that a son needs, so make sure he has many other great examples, i.e., a grandpa, uncle, teacher, coach, or family friends who are great role models.

"Does my son know that he matters to me?"

That depends on what you share together. Here are some ideas:

Read together, have learning time together, do errands and shopping with him.

- Work together in the garden.
- Shed tears for him when he's in trouble.
- Provide well for him.
- Discipline him well.
- Be a good example to him (most of the time).
- Be nurturing.
- Be guiding.
- Set rules.
- Set a good work example.
- Wait up for him.
- Show up on time.
- Do what you say.
- Finish what you start.
- Say please and thank you.
- And so on.

"Does my son know that I love him?"

- It will be easier if he sees:

- evidence I can be depended on,

- signs of my love,

- evidence of me as a protector,

- my strong will, tempered with fairness,

- me taking my provider/protector role seriously,

- my good example.

"Does my son know how proud I am of him?"

It will be easier if he sees:

- affirmation from me,

- evidence I am pleased with him for what he does well or wisely chooses not to do,

- evidence I am pleased with who he is.

That concludes our list. Now, back to our story. (See expanded list in Appendix B)

NORTHSIDE

About the time I was born, Dad bought three acres of land about two miles north of town. It started out to be a large garden/orchard to grow fruits and vegetables for his growing family and also a place for him to have a diversion to his busy business in town. At the same time it would allow him to exercise some of the farming skills that he learned on his father's farm in the old country.

I would like to believe that in addition to that, he also wanted to create a place to spend time with his three sons and teach them some of the principles of farming and the joy of good work habits that he learned from his father. At least that is how it looks to me these many decades later.

My dad named this Garden of Eden "Northside," but with his European accent it sounded more like, "Nort-side." So, almost every weeknight in the spring, summer, and fall, after eating a large meat-and-potatoes supper made by Mom, we, the boys, and my dad would pile into the 1941 Chevy two-door Custom Deluxe loaded with tools and supplies for two to three hours of good work. There would be plenty of digging, planting, weeding, and picking of fruits and vegetables for us boys, while my dad would be busy cutting down the grasses and weeds with his European scythe, which he had specially made in his homeland. If you are not sure just what a scythe looks like, just think of the one that the Grim Reaper is always seen with. That would be just like the one my dad spent hours with at Northside.

He was a master at swinging that scythe and he really made the grass and weeds fly. It must have given him much pleasure to work up a sweat using that implement, and I now realize that it must have reminded him of his days on the family farm in Slovenia, working with his own dad and brothers. I wish now that he had helped us make that connection to what we were then doing, but he didn't. At least, I don't remember it.

Though Northside was only three acres in size, Dad had planned it well. In the center area was a large plowed field where all of the family vegetables were grown.

You name it, it was there. From sweet corn and popcorn to tomatoes, onions, radishes, cabbage, pumpkins, potatoes, lettuce, and so forth. Around the perimeter would be large climbing trees for us boys, plus fruit trees that included several kinds of pear and apple trees, cherry trees. There were major grapevines, and strawberry and raspberry patches. It was a very unusual garden, well planned and very good at providing our family of seven with all the canned vegetables and fruits we would eat all year long. Mom was a master at that, and my sisters would help her.

My earliest memories of my first few trips to Northside as a very young boy, maybe three or four years old, were not about work. I was too little for that. I had a lot of fun, though, and I always seemed to get into trouble with my older brother and/or my dad. I remember that I ended up banished to sit in the '41 Chevy until the work was done. I waited for the customary trip to the Dairy Queen that followed our trips to Northside.

Sitting in the car by myself was boring. That is, until I discovered the neat accessory on the dash board called a cigar lighter! Wow! What fun. I found out if you just pushed it in for a short time it popped out with a red fire tip that was very hot! Now things started to get fun again. I found out that when the hot lighter popped out, I could burn these very cool circle designs in the felt upholstery on the doors, which I did numerous times before my dad checked on me and caught me burning holes in the car upholstery! No ice cream that day. I got a good spanking, too.

From then on, I was assigned the job of pulling weeds in the garden.

Looking back on all of those times at Northside, I now realize that that's where I learned the joy of good hard work. It was my dad's way of teaching us to be responsible, teaching us to enjoy working hard. Plus, there were many other connection points between father and sons during these trips to Northside.

Thanks, Dad, for taking the time to teach us those great values. To show your love for us in the way you did, to encourage, to discipline, and to show us your pleasure as we helped you work...and thanks, too, for all the fine trips to the Dairy Queen for cones on the way home. Those things will never to be forgotten.

THE BEACON

These memories and those of my father and me listening to The Greatest Stories Ever Told on the old Philco radio have become a beacon in my life, a source of light, guidance, good feeling. The radio times stand out in my mind for two reasons: first, because the connection we shared during those broadcasts was such a powerful and purposeful one, and second, more sadly perhaps, because it was so rare.

The reality was that my father and I had a lot of great memories, but we also failed to connect in many areas of my life. That weekly radio broadcast served, for a time, as a connection point, as something that meant as much to me as Northside. As I entered adolescence, that kind of connecting point between us vanished, and I came to feel more my father's absence in my life than his presence.

I've already told you that my dad was not an expressive man with his family in terms of emotional affection, and you may have picked up by now that this is actually a major understatement. He was tough and at times, quite disapproving when one felt the need for approval. I think one of the things that drew him to that weekly radio broadcast was that it expressed positive values to me and my siblings that he literally couldn't express himself. He simply didn't have the vocabulary or ability.

I've also told you that he was extremely devoted to his work. Today, in fact we might call him a workaholic. Back then, we called him a good provider. I suppose there is some truth to both labels. Whatever label we put on it, the reality of our lives was that he spent most of his time in his tailor's shop. We often didn't see much of him, even though he was only steps away.

When we add to the mix the fact that I was, just as he had been, a restless middle child who stood in the shadow the firstborn son, who always is the favorite in the classic European family, we can begin to see a recipe, not for connection, but for disconnection. That's what I began to experience as I got a little older, disconnection and the feeling of being alone. That feeling of disconnection and loneliness led to a great deal of pain, and I began looking around for ways to dull that pain.

THE GANG

I found one way to dull the pain—or I thought I did—with a rough gang of older boys, with whom I began drinking heavily at a very young age, probably around twelve or thirteen. There was a lot of talk in the newspapers during this period about a social problem called "juvenile delinquency." I suppose I was part of that problem. I do remember that, for the first two years of high school, we often imbibed either before or after school. In fact, the problem began well before that. I remember that at my eighth-grade graduation, a half a dozen of us walked across the stage to receive our diplomas with a strong smell of whiskey on our breath.

All my family knew was that I wasn't doing well in school, and that I had fallen in with a bad crowd. That was certainly true, and it was also true that I was in deep trouble, and my life was headed in a very bad direction. They didn't know how bad yet, and I don't think I did, either.

These were a bunch of rowdy guys that I hung out with. Most of them were older than I was. We all had problems at home of various kinds. In a way, our group kind of served as each guy's alternative family.

The instinct was understandable—it's the same instinct that drives problems with gangs in big cities today. When young men feel alienated and disconnected, and they don't have a lot of support from their families, then they reach out to each other for support. There's nothing wrong with any of that in theory, of course...but sometime the ways that guys find to support each other isn't really much support for anyone.

That's the way it was with my group. Our recreation was actually bad for us. I was a big part of making that recreation happen, as it turned out, because I knew how to drive, and I was big for my age—six foot one by the time I was thirteen. If I didn't talk much, people actually thought I was grown up. That meant I could get us to the liquor store (driving someone else's car, of course), and I could also pass for eighteen, which was how old you had to be back then to buy liquor. So I was a pretty useful guy to have around.

ALCOHOL

We drank a lot of beer, because beer was cheap. On special occasions—which is another way of saying, "when somebody had a few extra bucks" we drank whiskey. I never drank alone. I always drank with the guys. I felt at home with the guys.

My dad was not a drinker. In fact, except for an occasional glass of wine, alcohol was off limits in his house. Looking back, I think maybe that might have even been part of the reason it was important to me to spend as much time out drinking with the guys as I did.

We drank too much, and we did it most nights of the week. We drank at someone's house if we knew the parents were away. We drank in the car if we couldn't find anywhere else. Somehow, I was always the guy doing the driving, without a license, of course, and half the time I'd had too much to drink. Looking back now, I realize what a miracle it was that nobody got hurt or killed on those binge outings, but back in those days, we operated on the assumptions that nothing could happen to any of us, that we were invincible.

Maybe I didn't fit the clinical definition of an alcoholic, but by the time I was fourteen drinking with my friends had become a way of life for me. Ultimately, it was a sad way of life. It was a way of life that usually left you feeling terrible the next morning, but at least it always had a party you could look forward to, and a group that gave you a feeling of belonging somewhere. We raised a ruckus more or less every night, those guys and me. My grades had collapsed, and my family was growing more distant by the day, but at least I belonged somewhere— or so I thought.

TROUBLE ON THE HORIZON

I suppose there was, throughout these years, something inside me that knew, deep down, that what was happening between me and my friends most nights of the week wasn't going to last forever, and couldn't last forever, and for that matter probably shouldn't last forever. I suppose that part of me sensed that somehow, in some way, things were going to go wrong. Another part of me, though, just didn't want the party to stop.

There was a steadily expanding list of lies to our families, a long trail of illegal liquor purchases, petty theft, property damage of various minor, but escalating, varieties, and a general mutually encouraged appetite for troublemaking and fighting that was eventually going to get us noticed by somebody. My friends and I were courting trouble, and I knew it. But I didn't do anything about it.

I do remember wondering whether we were eventually going to find ourselves looking at some kind of serious problem with our parents, with the law, or with both at the same time, and if so, what the problem was likely to look like. I knew that most of what we were doing was against the law, and that all of what we were doing was against our families' wishes. But we kept right on doing it, because (as I have said) we got a sense of community from each other that we couldn't possibly get from any other source. Where would it all end?

Unfortunately, I now know all too well what happened in the end to most of the other guys in that circle of mine. None of them ended up having particularly happy lives; some of them wound up in prison. At least two of them died quite young. In the early fifties, I was spending time with people who (as my parents suspected) were part of what was then known as a bad crowd—a crowd on a collision course with disaster. I know now, having barely survived the wreckage myself, that membership in that kind of crowd exacts a heavy price.

Dead, in prison, or in a heap of trouble and about to get into some more was, from a strictly statistical standpoint, probably where I should've ended up, too. But I didn't, and the reason I didn't, as near as I can make out, had to be something I can't even define perfectly, even after all these years. But I will try to discuss here. That something is called the grace of God.

WHAT IS GRACE?

Grace is unexpected, grace is unwarranted, and grace is ample blessing to the repentant sinner from God the Father. Grace is more than we deserve. Grace is a second chance when we've already used up all of our second chances...and then some.

However you define it, I invite you to consider the possibility that opportunities for grace come our way every day. The only question is whether we notice them and act on them, or not. Sometimes it takes the experience of something truly terrible happening to us for us to recognize that we are looking at an opportunity to take advantage of grace. That's the way it was for me, at any rate.

I suspect grace is an individual blessing. It certainly was for me. The famous hymn "Amazing Grace" describes this deeply personal experience, the experience of getting far more than you deserve in terms of guidance, salvation, and forgiveness from God the Father. The song is so well known now, of course, and has been sung so often in so many different settings, that to some people it almost seems like a cliché. But it doesn't seem like a cliché to me because I was on the receiving end of that kind of grace, just as the man who wrote the song was. When it was written back in the late eighteenth century, it was a song of thanks to God the Father that came directly from the heart of a seaman who faced disaster and sought divine aid in overcoming it. He was a pilot named John Newton who, during an ocean voyage, encountered a furious storm that convinced him that death was near. He begged God for forgiveness for his past sins and for guidance through the storm. He received both and underwent a religious conversion that eventually led him into Christian ministry.

This song is really about turning around your own boat, your own life, with the aid of God the Father. That sea captain's words are far more powerful than any description I'll ever be able to bring to the task of defining grace, so I am taking the liberty of sharing the lyrics with you here.

The Falling-Out

Amazing Grace, how sweet the sound,

That saved a wretch like me...

I once was lost but now am found,

Was blind, but now, I see.

'Twas Grace that taught...

my heart to fear.

And Grace, my fears relieved.

How precious did that Grace appear...

the hour I first believed.

Through many dangers, toils and snares...

we have already come.

T'was Grace that brought us safe thus far...

and Grace will lead us home.

The Lord has promised good to me...

His word my hope secures.

He will my shield and portion be...

as long as life endures.

When we've been here ten thousand years...

bright shining as the sun.

We've no less days to sing God's praise...

then when we've first begun.

Amazing Grace, how sweet the sound,

That saved a wretch like me...

I once was lost but now am found,

Was blind, but now, I see.

Perhaps those words are familiar to you, but even if they are, rereading them may remind you, as it always reminds me, about the true meaning of grace. Grace is forgiveness and salvation from the Father, which you don't deserve but are offered anyway. And that is exactly what happened to me at the age of fifteen, when the deep trouble, which I had a feeling was on its way for my buddies and me, finally arrived.

OPPORTUNITY OF A LIFETIME?

I suppose that, as long as there have been beer-drinking boys driving around in cars, there have been dangers waiting for them at night. The big problem comes when danger begins to looks like opportunity.

The night when everything began to unravel for my buddies and me began like any other. It started with beer and plenty of it. My friends and I got together, I bought the beer, and we spent the better part of the evening drinking in the car on a secluded country road. Then we decided to devote the remainder of the night to driving around so we could see what was going on in the great, spinning world that lay before us.

As it turned out, what was going on in the outside world was, among other things, a large fire that had broken out at a sporting goods store in our town. High drama! We could see where flames had, not long before, been shooting out of some of the openings of the building. But everything was out now. A big front window had been broken somehow, probably by the firemen. I parked the car so we could take a look. As usual, I had been the one who was doing the driving that night. I was behind the wheel of my best friend's dad's Chevy.

Now, if you take a bunch of teenaged boys who have been drinking too much and show them a store that has caught fire, and then been extinguished, there are a couple of interesting things that may take place. If you've just had a really intense fire, and if the boys aren't particularly imaginative, they may just stare for a while in awe and wait for the fire department or the police to come back, as of course they will. But if you've got a group of real visionary thinkers like the ones that had gathered in my friend's dad's car that night, a whole different, and much more interesting, avenue for strategic planning develops: people start thinking about whether they should help themselves to the goods in the blackened store.

I can't remember whose idea that was, but I can remember that we all seemed to think it was brilliant.

WHAT COULD GO WRONG?

What difference did it make? All of the stuff in the store was going to be replaced by insurance money anyway. The fireman had secured the place. The police were nowhere to be seen.

What could possibly go wrong?

Through a back door that looked liked it must have been hacked open with the axes of the firemen, we made our way into the store and started helping ourselves to water-soaked, singed, and soot-covered pocket knives, catchers mitts, footballs, and other damaged things of interest to boys who had too much to drink and who imagined themselves lucky. We were having a grand time, laughing and joking and generally enjoying ourselves at the expense of the rest of the world, competing with one and another for who could pick out the most impressive stuff. It was the best night out yet. Until we saw the flashing red light and heard the words of someone, presumably someone in uniform, saying, "Police! All of you, stop where you are and turn around right now."

If there was any doubt in our minds or hearts about whether or not anything could possibly go wrong that night, well, that one concise, confidently delivered imperative sentence delivered from the mouth of a total stranger, whom we all somehow seemed to know intimately, removed the doubt instantly. There was also, it turned out, no doubt whatsoever in our hearts and minds about whether or not we wanted to be arrested. We all wanted to be out of there, in a hurry.

We ignored the officer's helpful instructions, dropped everything that we had gathered, turned, and ran for the back door like coon dogs that had just picked up the scent. We were out of the hacked-open back door in less than a second, and somehow, distracted as we were, things suddenly became quite clear for us. We all decided simultaneously, without a word, that our best chance for escaping disaster lay in abandoning the car and separating as quickly as possible. Each of us sped off on foot in a separate direction, fueled by the combustible mix of adrenaline, terror, night, and the looming possibility of being thrown in jail. I do not believe I have ever run any faster. I ran as only a teenage boy who knows trouble is right behind him can run.

I knew that, directly behind the department store, down a steep embankment, was a weed-filled body of water called the Illinois Michigan canal. This was something that had been built back in the early 1900s in order to connect Chicago to different cities in the Midwest. Back then, the canal had been the equivalent of what we would today call an interstate highway—only this highway didn't move cars and trucks; it moved barges. A whole lot of freight and people had once traveled that canal to get from LaSalle to Chicago and beyond, and then get back again. A road built alongside the canal had allowed horses to pull the barges. That was the transport system back then. If you wanted to, you could walk that road all the way from LaSalle to Chicago, whether you were a horse or not.

Things had changed a lot in half a century. Horses no longer stepped along those roads, and barges no longer brought cotton or newspapers or lumber from one point to another. Now, in the early fifties, the canal had become something very different. In fact, it was quite easy to tell just what it had become by the time I reached my fifteenth year. All you had to do was use your nose, and you could find it without a problem. The Illinois Michigan Canal was now an open sewer.

No longer needed as a freight artery, the canal had become a convenient place to dump waste, human and otherwise. Back then, people didn't much care where they dumped their waste, and companies didn't much care about the environmental impact of heaving all kinds of garbage, some of it pretty disgusting, into the canal. The once-proud highway of Midwestern commerce had become a river of muck, mire, and sewage. And it smelled to high heaven. Just a few seconds after I had bolted out the back door of the sporting goods store, I had picked up its distinctive scent, and I got an idea.

What was the last place in the world that anyone, even a police officer, would want to go scouting around in for an errant teen, in the middle of the night, who had clearly recognized the error of his ways?

The minute the thought crossed my mind, I knew the answer: the filth-filled waters of the Illinois Michigan Canal. I skidded down the embankment, closed my lips tight, held my nose, and got ready to take a swim.

MUCK AND MIRE

Before five seconds had passed, I was up to my chest in sewer water. Hunks of waste floated past me. The whole thing smelled awful. And now I did, too. But at least I was out of sight of the police.

A large auto bridge spanned the canal. Alongside the canal ran the tracks for the famous Rock Island Line, a railway famous locally and, eventually, internationally, thanks to a song about it written by

Leadbelly, and also sung by Johnny Cash. I found myself wishing, as I often did in those days, that I was on the train. But I wasn't. A few long moments went by and then: the worst sight in the world. Through the gloom, I could see what I was afraid I would see: three officers at the top of that bridge, shining the broad beams of three flashlights into the depths of the water. I quickly made my way, just as quickly as I could, over toward a bank that gave me cover behind some tall reeds. It seemed out of the way, although I was still chest deep in filth. At least here, I was offered a little bit of protection from the lights, although I wasn't sure how they could see much of anything in the strange darkness that surrounded us all that evening.

I was now surrounded not only by muck and mire, but by weeds and garbage. It was only a question of time. If the police decide to wait me out, if they called my bet, if they came wading into the filth to track me down, I was done for. It would be big trouble for me. On the other hand, if I was more patient than they were, if I was quiet, if I had bet right that they were unwilling to spend their time, their dignity, and their attention tracing down a wayward teenage boy in a river of filth, then I was safe.

They called from the bridge that there was no use for me to hide. They would find me sooner or later. "It will all be easier for you if you come out now and talk to us."

My heart pounded in my chest. I did something that moment that I cannot recall ever having done before: I prayed with all my heart for help from God the Father.

I suppose I had never been in a spot as difficult as this one before, and I suppose that what I was praying for—not to be punished for something clearly wrong, clearly illegal—was not all that noble. I suppose, too, that the fear in my heart was less fear of God than fear of what my father would say and do if he ever found out about the fix I had gotten myself into. Despite all of that, however, I prayed with every atom of my being for God to see me through this horrific emergency.

My prayer was for help from God the Father, if he was really there. I was honest enough to admit that moment that I didn't really know. I pleaded for an answer anyway. His clear answer to me, in my hiding place in the muck and mire, was not in words, but in thoughts planted into my very being. I prayed for a way forward. If only he would make me safe in this terrible situation, I promised, I would vow never to fall this far again, and I would strive to be a better son, a better Christian, and a better person—a better anything—as long as I could get out of these weeds tonight without going to jail. To my astonishment, I heard an answer, not audible to others, perhaps, but audible in my heart and my mind.

His words were, "Take my hand," and I understood those words perfectly.

THE OTHER VOICE

But then at the same time, another thought entered my mind. It was an opposing voice, an oppressive voice, a voice that told me, "There is no hope. You are no good. You are lost. You have failed your family."

That negative voice pulled me down. I felt doomed and hopeless. I could feel myself slipping down further into the quicksand of my life.

Then I heard again these words from the Father God. "Take my hand!"

I did—and I held on tightly!

Years later, I learned from a missionary friend of mine that the opposing voice is always present in our minds, always trying to drag us down, always trying to get us to stray from the Spirit of God. It is the voice of Sarx, the Greek word that can be translated as "flesh," or "the evil one," or "our old nature."

This same missionary friend explained further that we must choose whom we will listen to in life. He used the illustration of the Continental Divide: If we stand at the peak of the Divide and pour water down one side of it, it will flow to the Atlantic Ocean. If we choose to pour it down the opposite side, it will flow to the Pacific. It's all a matter of which direction we choose.

In the same way, we each must choose who we will listen to in life: the voice that leads to the way of life, meaning God the Father, the Holy Spirit, Jesus Christ, and eternal life with God—or the way of death, meaning Sarx: the evil voice within us that leads to death, sin, and hell.

This verse of scripture perfectly summed up my experience that evening:

... He turned to me and heard my cry. He lifted me out of the slimy pit, out of the muck and mire; he set my feet on a firm place to stand. He put a new song in my mouth, a hymn of praise to our God. Many will see and fear the lord. And put their trust in him. Blessed is the one who trusts in the lord. (Psalm 40:1-4)

THE TURNING POINT

This, I knew, was a major event in my life. I was tired of my foolish ways and the path that brought me to this horrible place. I was ready to listen, to pray more about my condition...for help from God, to become the person that he wanted me to be.

At that moment, I knew that God existed. Truth be told, I don't exactly remember everything I promised God that dark night, there in the depths of the muck and mire, but I do remember knowing for certain that I had reached a turning point. I had to turn things around. If I somehow got out of this, I had to make sure things changed.

When the police gave up and walked off the bridge, my heart leaped, and it seemed to me that my prayer had been answered. It had been, but like many prayers, it was answered in a way that took a while for me to understand. At the moment, all I knew was that I was free. Smelly, wet, and exhausted, but free.

I was black with sewage, covered head to foot in filth. After taking a short cleansing dip, clothes and all, in the clean running water of a nearby creek, I felt strangely refreshed, in body, mind, and spirit, as I found my way home that evening.

I have said that my prayer that night was answered, and looking back across the years, I can attest that it certainly was. God did hear my prayer, and he did make a new way forward for me, a way that led to a different kind of life, a brighter pathway than the darker and dangerous one I was traveling.

FACING THE MUSIC

I should also be clear, however, that the very next day led me to an outcome that definitely was not what I prayed for. My most immediate hopes—those of not getting in trouble, not having to face up to my father over what I had done—were going to be dashed.

Yet I would be wrong to say that I was angry at God about this turn of events, or that my sense of purpose had been shaken. I was angry at myself when it became clear that I was to face the music. I knew what I had heard in my heart—"Take my hand"—and I felt quite confident in doing so. I was a little unsure, though, about what exactly I was supposed to do next, especially when I saw the police car pull up in front of our house the next day.

I had prayed they would not take me. Some of the poets make the point—and a few country singers as well—that some of God's greatest gifts are unanswered prayers. I know this to be true now, but it wasn't quite as obvious to me when I was on the brink of my sixteenth birthday, staring out the window. I had imagined I was free, but the police had come for me. I had no idea how they had tracked me down, but they did.

I learned later that someone in our group who had not gotten away, and who had been arrested that night, gave the police the names of all those who had been involved in the trespassing and looting. My name was on that list. This was the most immediate answer to the question: Why is a squad car driven by two of LaSalle's finest in front of our home? They had gotten a hot tip from someone in our group—an accurate tip—that I was one of the looters, and they'd been sent to pick me up and escort me back to the station. I remember thinking I would have probably given up the names, too, if I had been the one who'd been caught.

THE LONG RIDE HOME

I no longer remember why my father wasn't around at the time I was arrested. I suppose he was off on an errand somewhere. What I do remember were the tears on his face when he came to the jail to pick me up later that day.

This was everything I had prayed wouldn't happen, and I was crushed, mostly because I knew how deeply my dad was being humiliated. It was not what I had intended. All of the behavior problems, all of my rebellion, had led to this, an Old-World man, a man who saw himself (rightly) as one of the pillars of the community, a man who knew and was known by virtually everyone in our town, had been left with a deep and enduring sense of shame because of his wayward son—because of me.

He took me home, but no words were spoken. I knew I had broken his heart. I had brought dishonor on the house, and things might never again be the same between us.

THE WALL

That business about bringing dishonor to the house was no joke. My father was an old-school man, a European man, a man who built his family, his business, and indeed his whole life around the idea of principled behavior. He was a stand-up guy, a man who worked hard, a man whose words could be trusted. And now he was the father of a common thief. He was the father of a juvenile delinquent. For me to have done what I did was beyond shameful. It was a kind of setback similar to what he might have experienced if he had a heart attack or learned of a death in the family. It took something out of him, something very serious indeed. And the disgrace I brought him that day was a big part of the reason that such an impenetrable wall between us emerged, a wall that would take years to overcome.

At first I thought that I was going to have to go to reform school. That, I knew, would be yet another blot upon the family name, and a considerable blow to my father as well, considering how much of my father's business relied on positive word-of-mouth referrals.

When the police explained the seriousness of the situation to my father, and when he later explained it to my mother, a fog of desperation, silence, and bitterness settled over our family. The loving heart of my dear mother was a great comfort to me during these difficult times.

I will always be thankful for that. But I know this time was hard on her.

It's hard to describe how terrible each moment in that house felt, how strained our dinner conversations were, how painfully the glances from my mother and siblings stung me. I did not have to deal with my father's glances, because he no longer met my eyes, but somehow that was even worse. And yet I did not feel any sense of panic.

It's hard to explain precisely why, but even the possibility of being sent to reform school —which was about as low as your fortunes could get in the midfifties in LaSalle, Illinois, if you happened to be a teenager—really did not terrify me now. I expected to be terrified. I expected to feel frightened and traumatized, expected to feel the urge to do something desperate, like run away from home. But after that moment when I heard the voice in my heart saying, "Take my hand," all I really felt was calm. I was certainly curious to learn what was going to happen next, but I was also quite certain that I was being led in the right direction by something or someone.

Events later proved that the sense of confidence that I had, the trust that I would be led to the right place, was not misplaced.

ROSE TO THE RESCUE

Just a few days later, out of nowhere, not deserving it, not expecting it, I received a call from my older sister, Rose.

Rose was fourteen years older than me, and she was married to a doctor, Gene. She wanted to know if I would be interesting in staying with her and her husband for a while at their home in suburban Chicago. Just when it became clear that I was in real trouble, the opportunity emerged to change my home environment. It seemed like a better option than going to reform school.

The decision to spend some time with my sister meant putting some physical distance between me and my parents. There was significant emotional distance there already. There would now be a little geographical distance as well. My sister was a wise woman, and she sensed that a change of environment would do me good at this point in my life.

She had heard my story from my mom and called to make an amazing offer to her wayward younger brother. "Come to live with us. Leave behind all the bad experiences and get a fresh start in a positive environment."

My mind immediately shot me back to the time, just days before, in that filthy canal. I had made my desperate plea to God the Father for help. Again, I heard words in my mind and heart. This time it said, "You need to go."

I accepted her offer.

PART FOUR

Reconciliations

THE ROCK ISLAND LINE

Just a few days later, I was on the 7:00 a.m. train, the Rock Island Rocket, on my way to a new life in the Chicago area. As the train pulled away from the station, I looked out the window... and got a glimpse of the canal where I had my first talk with God the Father! My eyes got a little misty, and a thin smile crossed my face as I fully realized I was no longer alone in this great adventure called life.

As the last of the familiar scenery flew past my rain-streaked window, I thought of the lyrics of one of my dad's favorite songs by Doris Day: Que sera, sera; whatever will be, will be; the future's not ours to see, que sera, sera. No, we may not know our future...but I think now that I do know who holds our future: God the Father.

Two hours later, I was standing alone, a fifteen-year-old kid, in the huge marble-floored waiting room of Chicago's LaSalle Street station. Even the name seemed like part of a plan. It was just me, along with a small cardboard suitcase that was filled with some clothes and a few extras. I felt very small, but somehow at peace.

THE HARMONICA MAN

My sister Rose would not be able to pick me up until much later in the afternoon, so I had some time to kill in the very large train station set into the heart of the very large city of Chicago. I was getting hungry, but I only had one dollar and some change in my pocket, along with the beat-up old harmonica that I always carried. After eating a big sweet roll (twenty cents), I started to explore the station.

Inside, it was a beehive of people, all walking fast, probably to work. Outside, it was a sea of cars, cabs, and wall-to-wall commuters, all on their way someplace, fast. I noticed the street people in front of the train station. Some of them were begging for money, some were just sitting there, and several were making music, either by singing or by playing an instrument. They were all hoping to get some tip money for their performances. There was one man playing the accordion, another playing the saxophone, and a good-looking black man who was strumming on a guitar and playing the harmonica simultaneously. He had one of those neck-brace things that hold the harmonica in place. He was very good, and he was getting some money.

I took my cue from him. I said, "Hey, I can do that!" It seemed like a great way to make some fast money while I waited. Who knew? It might even turn into a full-time job for me. I found a place to stand and started playing my harmonica. I put an old tin cup on top of my cardboard suitcase. That was to hold the money I would soon be receiving.

I played for three or four hours. Only a few people stopped. After all that time, there were just a few small coins in the can. I began to wonder about the wisdom of my moneymaking idea. Also, I noticed that the black guitar player had been watching me struggle. After a while, he came over to me and said, "Hey, boy, you got someplace to go?"

I said, "Maybe."

"Then you'd better get on your way there," he said. "You'll starve out here on the street. You get yourself some schooling, son. Grow up some. Learn how to play that harmonica right. And you listen to your father!"

I said, "Okay."

"Go on now," he continued. "Get!"

I did. I began gathering my things. Before I could grab the tin cup, he reached into his pocket and dropped four silver quarters into it.

"Now get going!" he barked.

I thanked him again and started to make my way back into the station. Before I went in, I turned for one more look at the stranger who had sent me on my way, but he was gone in just seconds. I don't know who he was or what became of him. The one thing I do know is that he could play a really mean harmonica. Maybe, just maybe, he was an angel, sent to look after me.

Back inside the station, I saw my sister Rose walking toward me across the huge waiting area with a big smile on her face and her arms open for a hug.

A ROCKY FIRST VISIT

It would probably be a more pleasant and simpler story if I were able to say that I immediately felt as though I fit right in her household. The truth is actually quite different. The first week I spent with Rose and

Gene left me feeling somewhat disoriented, especially the experience of going to church. Church had not been part of my reality up to that point at all. I don't remember the details; I just remember feeling completely out of place.

It was a confusing time for me, and I was not used to making such big changes. After a week or so with my sister and her husband, I announced that I wanted to go home. I didn't say so; I don't think I could have said so, but I suspect that the emotional personal nature of what I experienced at the first church service had been a little overwhelming. Again, I don't recall anything specific that set me off. I just recall deciding that I didn't feel like who I was expected to be: too prim, too proper.

My sister and I had been out of touch for some time. And so, despite the fact that I knew that I was supposed to be on a different course in my life, I made the decision to head back to LaSalle. I told Rose what I wanted to do, and she arranged for my train trip back.

Almost immediately after making it back to my father's tailor shop, however, I wondered whether I had done the right thing.

YOU CAN'T GO HOME AGAIN

I had expected that there would be some friction with my family upon my return from my sister's house. And I was right on that. My father and I shared only monosyllables, and my mother's heart was clearly broken, which made me want to keep my distance. It was a really tense atmosphere, as I knew it would be. What I hadn't expected, through, was the very different relationship I would have with the guys in my former circle.

Before the night of the fire and the police chase, when I had almost been caught looting, I had felt as though I had almost everything in common with these fellows. Once I made it back from Chicago, though, it suddenly seemed as though we came from different planets. There was a distance between us now, a distance that I had not predicted, but that was impossible to deny.

I tried to explain to one of my buddies exactly what had happened to me that night. How my life changed, how his could change, too, how I had made a decision, and how things were going to be different. I actually tried to talk about religion with him, about the experience I had at my sister's place; he looked at me as if I had gone crazy. I suppose, from his point of view, I had.

Even the other kids I knew around the neighborhood presented a major obstacle to me, as well as a reminder that the life I had once lived was now gone forever. I hadn't noticed it before, but it became obvious just a few days after I made it home: they were not who I wanted to be. Before, they had seemed like the best people, the smartest guys, the best role models...but now they just seemed like people I didn't want to spend my time with. It didn't take me long to realize that I no longer fit in with the lifestyle I had known in LaSalle, Illinois. At first I thought my friends had changed, but I soon realized that I had become a different person.

A VOICE IN MY HEART

That voice in my heart started speaking up once again. It told me that I had missed out on my opportunity I needed to make a positive change in my life. It told me that there was nothing positive for me here, that I had been tempted to go back to an easier time in my life, but that I could not go home again. That time no longer existed. I had to make a new way for myself and follow a brand-new path, the path that had been laid out for me so clearly that night when I found myself cowering beneath the bridge.

A day or so after I made it back to LaSalle, Illinois, I began to listen to that voice.

I called my sister. I told her that I had made a terrible mistake, and I literally begged her to let me come and stay with her and her husband once more. This time, I promised, I would make it work.

It didn't take long for her to agree. (It was actually about ten seconds...the time it took her to tell her husband the reason for my call.)

THE RIDE BACK TO ROSE'S

The next day I found myself in the car with my brother-in-law, Gene. He was driving back toward Chicago, this time for keeps. I had a powerful sense that a whole new life awaited me. I was sure he thought I was some kind of head case, changing my mind the way I had.

The truth was that I had needed to work through the moment of uncertainty. I needed to test my choices in order to know what I was supposed to do next. I had to make the trip back to LaSalle. It hadn't been a mistake. I hoped he understood.

As we drove back, I told him how grateful I was. I told him that I was now sure that I felt God's hand working in my life. I also told him that I felt very strongly that letting me find out for myself where I belonged had been part of the divine plan. To my surprise, he agreed.

"Well, you did the right thing," he told me. "You did the right thing by going back to LaSalle, and you did the right thing by calling us yesterday to say you'd changed your mind. You were right both times, Tom."

"You knew that already?"

"Of course. Otherwise you would have doubted whether you were ready for this, because you would never have made sure for yourself whether you belonged with your old crowd. Now you know you don't belong with them. Right?"

"Right."

Gene and I had not gotten off to a very good start during my first visit. In fact, it's probably fair to say that we had done a pretty good job of getting on each other's nerves. We were very different people, Gene and I. He was reserved and analytical, and I was more spontaneous and likely to be unpredictable. His whole domestic life, including a strong marriage to my sister was about to change...and all because of a goofy teenager who talked a lot and seemed to get into trouble. Yet all those challenges seemed to evaporate now.

We had a good long talk in the car on the long ride to Chicago, and we hit it off a lot better the second time around. Once I took the time to listen to him, I realized that I actually liked him. He was, I realized, a very sensible man: mature, and professional. I opened up during that drive and told him I had made a terrible mistake with my old gang, that I knew Chicago was the best place for me, and that I was grateful they had agreed to let me try again. I also said, once again, that I was sure that I was going where God wanted me to be, and that I was ready to do whatever it took to become a better person.

By the time we got back to his house, he and I made peace. I had essentially the same talk with my sister, who was happy to see me. She was a wise woman, and she knew from experience how to get me back on track.

I wanted them both to know that I was totally on board. My attitude now was, "Show me what to do, tell me what you need." I knew I had to make this work.

News of my move to my sister Rose's place the first time was initially not well received in LaSalle, especially by my father. Even so, things went surprisingly well the second time around. A lot of people back home couldn't quite believe it when my sister called with her weekly status reports.

The words that God was placing in my mind and heart now were, "Study and work hard."

THE SPIRIT OF ADOPTION

When I left home at fifteen to live with my older sister and her husband, they took me on as part of the family. I almost felt like they had adopted me as their own son.

I was a wayward young man at that point in my life. I was failing at life, and I was lost, fearfully lost, but I prayed to the Father in a simple prayer: "Help me, Father God."

His clear answer to me was always: "Take my hand." And I did, holding on with all my might as if my very life depended on it. And it did! This was the beginning of my adoption by God the Father.

When I took His hand, I began to follow him, listen to him, obey him. Over a six-year period, I walked with God. Most of the time learning about his ways, with my hand in his, but sometimes I dropped his hand and went my own way. When I did, I always went back to my old ways and my old thinking. Fortunately, my sister Rose and her husband, Gene, were usually nearby to set me back on course. I learned a lot, but I also fell back into old ways often. However that happened less and less frequently over time.

During those years, Rose and Gene were very much like my surrogate parents. But later in my spiritual walk, when I put my faith and trust in Jesus Christ alone and asked him to be my Father God, he adopted me and became God the Father to me.

BACK ON TRACK

Everything came together. Don't ask me how, but it did. I went to church and to Bible study regularly with my sister and her husband, and what had so recently felt strange and difficult suddenly felt like something that was designed to make me come alive. I'm not saying that I had become the perfect Christian overnight. There were a lot of stumbles, a lot of falls, a lot of get-back-up moments, and a lot of brushings-off to come, as you shall see. But I was in the right environment. I had stopped drinking. And I was going to summer school to make up the work I had neglected. There was quite a lot of it. But for the first time in my memory, I was actually enjoying the process of going to class. I had a part-time job, too, working in a furniture store. I was enjoying that also.

Before I knew it, it was September and time for school to start up again. Now I had my sister and her husband telling me everyday about reaching my potential and striving to do my best in school. And I heard myself agreeing with them—that was my goal. I found myself reporting to a big-city high school for the very first time. Talk about culture shock. I was used to being a notable underachiever at a small-town high school of 500 kids, and every single one was white. The high school I was to attend had nearly 5,000 kids, a third of them black. I had never encountered another culture before, and I had a lot of adjusting to do.

Something about the change energized me. I can't say exactly what it was, but I can tell you that I immediately got interested in succeeding in school and creating new relationships there, in a way that I had never imagined possible. There can certainly be great power in a fresh start; I know this, because I experienced it first-hand that autumn. I remember saying to my sister, "I never knew school could be fun like this!" I meant it.

Suddenly I was doing well. I was working day and night, but I really didn't mind. I was headed in the right direction. I got very active socially and became involved with a group of good kids I knew in the school and church environments.

I neglected to mention an important piece of the story, which was that when my move to my sister's house was complete, I got an important piece of family news: I was about to become an uncle. My sister was pregnant.

It may have been the sense of starting over, the feeling that I was part of a new kind of family. It may have been the chance to take advantage of a different way of looking at my role in the family. It may have been a simple change in surroundings. Or it may have been, as I sensed in my heart, the direction of God the Father.

Whatever had brought the change about, I was now on a new path.

LEADER AND FOLLOWER

As I have mentioned, I found myself, to my astonishment, a leader in my youth group at church, in academics, in sports. And at home I found myself a follower: eager to do anything and everything necessary to make things right for my sister and her husband. We figured out each other's rhythms pretty quickly—I figured that we had to, with a baby on the way—and as a result of that willingness to follow, I found myself leading a whole new life. I was grateful.

The more time passed, the more obvious it became to me that I had made it past a fearful abyss. I realized now that the guys in the circle I had escaped from in LaSalle not only weren't my best friends, they weren't even friends at all. They were a loosely woven bunch of troubled guys. They didn't care about me. I had to think about all that I had gone through to realize that. Once I understood that, I never looked back.

I knew I had a steep road ahead of me, but I had my sister and my brother-in-law to help me keep on the straight path. They did that, first and foremost, by making sure I was always busy. I had my job in a furniture store, which was important because I now had to help support the household. I had to pay a modest monthly rent, and I had to buy my own clothes. You might imagine that those restrictions would have bothered me, and they certainly would have back in LaSalle, but in my sister's home I was okay with working and paying my way. After all, that's what my dad did. I felt like I was contributing, even if I wasn't.

Work, I began to realize, was a good learning experience, and I came to like it, just as I came to like school and church.

The next fateful year, the year that I finally began to turn my life around, was only possible because of the values of service and giving that my sister and her husband instilled in me.

Case in point, baby-sitting: something I never would have volunteered for back in LaSalle. When my sister's baby came, I helped to take care of her.

Her name was Joy. And I learned a whole lot about her during that first year of her life. It was odd caring for her, baby-sitting, and just hanging out together and giving her bottles, but this was something I hadn't expected. This was something totally unexpected, being called upon to help out in the care of my niece. I had spent so much time dealing with my own feelings, expressed or otherwise, about my father, that I didn't realize how much I stood to gain by helping to provide something that seemed an awful lot like parental care for someone else. I felt like I belonged.

Being one of three people responsible for overseeing a new life was exhausting and exciting, and it helped me to grow as a person. There is a prayer of St. Francis that says something to the effect that "it is in giving that we receive," and this was certainly the case for me. Helping my sister and her husband to bring this helpless baby up right also ended up doing a world of good for me. And it helped me to make the transition to the next stage of my own life.

JOY

I should explain here that my sister was a career woman. She stayed with Joy full time during the critical early months, although she got a lot of help from both me and Gene. A little before Joy's first birthday, my sister went back to work—which meant that any free time I had on the weekends and during the evenings became Joy time. And it was a joyous time for me. I certainly wasn't the only person caring for Joy, fixing her dinner and reading her stories, but I became her favorite Uncle Tom.

I wasn't the parent in this situation; my sister and her husband were very responsible, and they got their time in with Joy. But I was her uncle, and the two of us really bonded in all the good ways you can think of. We got along famously, and I got some understanding of what a great blessing it is to be a supporting family member in the life of a young person. Her favorite dinner, and mine, too, I remember, was Uncle Tom and Joy's famous "cowboy soup"—beans and cut-up hot dogs. It may not sound good, but we loved it.

I recall that I spent a lot of time reading Joy the storybooks she liked. We did a lot of reading in a large lighted closet that became our magical story room. It was kind of like entering our own special magical world. What's meaningful to me now is that I told a lot of my dad's stories to her in that reading room, which kind of brought things full circle. Joy became the little sister that I never had. We became pals as I read to her all the children's books that I never read as a child.

We read books and Bible stories, sang songs together, and did crafts, also. I had done none of those things as a small boy, but I loved doing them with Joy. Looking back, I know now that those experiences, too, were gifts from God. God was giving me a taste of the Christian childhood and storybooks that I never had as a child. Maybe that's why we both enjoyed these activities as much as we did.

By the time I was about seventeen years old, I often got to cook for Joy—if her parents were out for that evening. My other specialties: frozen chicken pot pies, fish sticks, and the best scrambled eggs this side of the Mississippi.

It was the most unlikely alliance a former teenaged troublemaker could have imagined. Joy and I just had a grand time together, and it dawned on me that I was able to fill some of the big gaps in my own life by helping to bring her up as her Uncle Tom. We became quite close.

AN UNLIKELY TEACHER

Around the same time, I began to take a more active role in the church youth group activities. I even started teaching Sunday school for the fourth-graders. Once again, the reality of having responsibility for someone younger and less experienced than myself was a real eye-opener. I can't say I was academically prepared for the job, or that I had any credentials necessary to do it well; in fact, most of the time I was only a page ahead of what the fourth-graders were supposed to be learning. But we all seemed to get along, and we all grew and learned from the experience. I was on the right path.

I had a whole lot of work to do. The time sped by. I had come a long way from the horrible moment beneath the bridge, wading through the sewage of my own self-absorption. And the key to turning my life around (I see now) had not been receiving, but rather giving.

The story gets a little more complicated and a lot more powerful for me as I recall it now. It seems unlikely to me as I look back on it, because my hands were as full as I thought they could get, but my apprenticeship as a dad-in-training got a bit more demanding about this time.

Years passed. I felt comfortable with the idea that Joy and I were family. That Rose and Gene were family, too. That I could feel close to these people, that I belonged here with them, and that we could count on each other. It was a good feeling. But it was hard not to feel a little disconcerted when my sister came home from work one day, sat down to dinner, and told me that my job was about to get three times bigger. The family was about to expand, and Rose and Gene needed my help.

I thought my sister was about to tell me she was pregnant again, but that wasn't it.

THE BOYS

Rose explained that she and Gene had decided to adopt two boys, ages nine and eleven, as their sons. This was a totally new development, and it came at me out of the blue. At first, I didn't know how to feel.

The boys were named Tommy and Steve, and they came from a troubled home. Their dad had been a high-school buddy of Gene's—I don't even recall his name now—and he was, my sister explained, in a bad way. We needed to find a way to help. The poor man had lost his wife to cancer, and that painful event had pushed him over the edge. He had a drinking problem, and he'd gone through a nervous breakdown. He was having a hard time bouncing back, and the family was in trouble.

I had met him briefly. I remember thinking that the alcohol had gotten the better of what had once been a very smart individual, and I remember feeling grateful that alcohol had not ruined my life, too. I remember thinking, too, that he was in no condition to take care of three boys.

The oldest son, Allen, was a teenager, and he had decided to enlist in the Marine Corps. The two younger boys, however, needed our help. Rose made the point—although she didn't have to—that even though I had not faced the problem of a family member being an alcoholic, I must surely remember what it meant to be in trouble and to need a helping hand.

She was right. I did remember that.

Now Rose's question was a simple one. Was I willing to start giving something back to some kids who needed help just as badly as I had a few years ago?

I told her I was. And I meant it. I had signed on to do whatever I could to help, and I planned to keep my word. I learned a lot about patience, support, and love for your brother, when I got two of them to deal with—more or less overnight.

FULL HOUSE

Suddenly we were a very full house, and my responsibilities had gotten substantially larger. But somehow it felt right, as though God were guiding me once again to exactly where I needed to go. And I believe he was. Just in case I haven't made it clear, my sister had a heart as big as a mountain, and she and Gene helped many needy people over the years by providing a safe haven for them when they needed it. Obviously, I was one of those people, and Tommy and Steve were the next in line. There were many more who came and went over the years, too many to list here. We used to joke about living at "Rose Hotel," but the reality was that Tommy and Steve were members of the family now, and I had a lot to do.

We were like a little military outfit, and I became the first sergeant in charge of the younger members of the family. After all my restlessness with my dad's brisk parenting style, I found myself using a lot of his no-nonsense vocabulary in dealing with the three kids, especially Tommy and Steve. There really wasn't any choice. Ours was not a huge house; there were three bedrooms. One was Rose and Gene's; one was Joy's; and what had been my bedroom now became a bedroom for the three of us boys. We stuffed three twin size beds in there.

THE BARRACKS

It was more like a barracks than a bedroom. My job each morning was to call out reveille, push the two guys out of bed, and get the day started. It was tough. Having practiced being a big brother for Joy, I had inherited two little brothers in order to show I was up for the job. And I think I was.

These two little guys had been through a lot, what with losing their mom and watching their dad unravel. They were often afraid, and Rose reminded me regularly that our first job was making them understand that their new family wasn't going to fall apart in a week. They were both very bright kids, and I realize now that I picked up just as many life lessons from them as they did from me. Tommy was the radical, the agitator of the two, the one who was trying to find a way to get under your skin. Dealing with that was a new experience, and very different indeed from dealing with Joy. I became the stern uncle, a role I learned to play quickly, because I was with them and running the platoon whenever Rose and Gene were out of the house. There was a whole lot of learning for all of us along the way. One night, as I was preparing a familiar dinner that Joy and I loved, scrambled eggs, little Tommy announced that he couldn't eat eggs. I saw this as a game. He played a lot of strange games—or perhaps this was just one of his latest attempts to get on my nerves.

It was time, I decided, to draw a line. I looked him in the eye and told him plainly, "Tommy, you're going to eat the same thing we are all eating, or you're not going to eat anything."

He told me that he wasn't going to eat anything then.

At this point, my patience reached its end. I sat down and pretty much forced him to eat the scrambled eggs that I had prepared. I felt certain that he was just messing with me, trying to show some kind of disrespect. How wrong I was. The poor guy really did have a deep aversion to eating eggs, almost a phobia, and he threw up the first few bites within seconds after having gulped them down on my orders. First sergeant or not, I learned to be a little gentler with everybody after that.

ROSE'S LEGACY

I'm not sure what happened to their older brother, the one who went into the Marines, but I do know that Tommy and Steve turned the corner. Despite their losses, they each had what appeared to be well-adjusted childhoods after they came to stay with us, and they each turned out to be more or less functional, contributing adults as a result of their stay at the Rose Hotel. How different their lives could have been if they had been sent to an institution. That was what they had been facing. If Rose had not intervened on their behalf, as she had intervened on mine, who knows what kind of trouble they could have gotten into?

I credit Rose for all three of us making it through.

THE CHEERLEADERS

Somehow, after two years and a little more of summer school, with plenty of extra classes to make up for all the class time I had missed back in LaSalle, I had graduated from high school, something I never would have predicted back when I was cutting classes and drinking beer every day. My sister and her husband were very proud, and although I still lived at my sister Rose's house, they began stepping back from the quasi-parental role that they had assumed and became my two biggest cheerleaders. They trusted me. They told me I was on the right track. And I was, thanks to them, and to God.

It was time for me to figure out what I was going to do with my life. Somehow I knew that my career goal in life was to start a business, as Dad had. He'd always had two big sayings about work. He said, "Find a job and make it better," and he also said, "If you don't have a job, make one, and make it the best it can be." The second path was the one I wanted to follow.

Dad and I had remained in contact, of course, and I knew that this goal of mine pleased him, even though we did not live together now. The truth was that, having come out of my dark period; I still respected my father enormously, and wanted to live up to his example. I could tell he was happy that I decided to follow in his footsteps and become an entrepreneur—a plugger, as he would have put it. In the world that I lived in, though, and with the talents and interests that I had, I knew that my path was not going to involve buying a storefront and starting a tailor's shop.

THE ZOMBIE YEARS

My goal was to start my own company, and I knew that in order to do that, I needed both an education and experience. I wanted to get that education just as quickly as I could, so I decided that I would catch up on the basic courses I needed at a local liberal arts college, and then move on to my business instruction at a larger business school. I came to call this period in my life—the period when I was taking college-level and eventually graduate-level courses at the same time I was holding down both a full-time and a part-time job—the zombie years. I was tired all the time, but I loved it.

I have to share here that my approach to business education was pragmatic. It had to be, given my time commitments. I was more interested in getting the information I needed than in getting formal credit. By this time I moved on to Northwestern University's Chicago campus and was happy to get the courses I needed. I never got a formal degree from Northwestern, but I sure did learn a lot there. Most of the instructors were either executives at publicly held companies, or entrepreneurs who ran their own firms. This was practical, real-world stuff, and I took in as much as I could—between my shifts as a buyer for a national purchasing company and as a worker at a furniture outfit.

Before long, I was part of a crowd of wannabe-entrepreneurs at Northwestern. We called ourselves the Moguls, and though a lot of us were auditing some of our courses, we acted like we were a fraternity. We even had a frat pin made up, though the idea of being a real fraternity was contradicted by the presence of a couple of female Moguls. I recall a lot of Friday night meetings at a local campus bar where we all shared our hopes and dreams of launching our own companies. For me, I knew that path lay in the world of sales and marketing. That, I had decided, was where I was going to get my real-world experience: generating revenue. Once I had that down, I would start my own company.

After two years at the local liberal arts college and two years of getting everything I could possibly get from Northwestern, I decided that there was no longer much point in sticking around auditing classes. About half of the moguls had reached the same conclusion, and we dropped out.

The zombie years were over. It was time to start turning my dream into reality.

We moguls all shared one common thought—that we needed some real life business experience. For me, that meant the world of sales and marketing, and a business that I could learn from, or either buying or starting a new business from scratch.

Everything that I learned in business school—and from my dad, who started and ran his own business for fifty-five years—told me that was to be my goal.

STUMBLING

I would like to be able to tell you that having experienced the healing force and the forgiveness of the Father God in my own life, my own path forward was a straight and confident one, it had no uphill paths, and I never stumbled. But if I told you that, I wouldn't be telling you the truth, and the whole reason I started this project was to get down the true experience of my own ongoing journey toward reconciliation, both with my own father and with the Heavenly Father who patiently guides us all.

The truth is, I stumbled along the way, and I had to stop and get my bearings more than once. I'm not glad that I stumbled, of course, but I am very glad indeed that God Almighty continued to see fit to point me in the right direction at the most critical points in my life.

Those experiences of stumbling through important decisions, of needing forgiveness and seeking it, and of hearing the guiding voice of God the Father (at least seven or eight different times over a six-year period) telling me what I needed to do next, brought home to me the vital importance of forgiveness, both toward members of my own family and towards others in my life. Recently I came across a quote from Mother Teresa that captured this perfectly.

> *People are often unreasonable and self-centered. Forgive them anyway. If you are kind, people may accuse you of ulterior motives. Be kind anyway. If you are honest, people may cheat you. Be honest anyway. If you find happiness, people may be jealous. Be happy anyway. The good you do today may be forgotten tomorrow. Do good anyway. Give the world the best you have and it may never be enough. Give your best anyway. For you see, in the end, it is between you and God. It was never between you and them anyway.*

There is another important saying, a saying about two paths: the narrow, difficult path that leads to salvation, and the broad, easy-to-travel path that leads to losing yourself and your soul forever. My theory, which I take from that saying, is that what matters most is not whether we go astray in life, but whether we are able to realize in time that it's important for us to get back on the straight path.

This next part of the book is a testimony of gratitude. At the most important moments of my young adult years and the years that followed, I was guided back to the path that I was meant to travel. I was and am grateful for God's hand on my life, and his great mercy and grace.

A CHANGE IN PLANS

In July 1962, I was eager to get my career on the fast track, but Uncle Sam interrupted my plans. I found out that I was about to be drafted. My draft number had gotten me to the top of the list. I saw military service as a major interruption of two years to my entrepreneurial plans. At the last minute I found what I thought was a better answer. I joined the Army National Guard. It was a six year obligation, but only six months of active duty at the beginning followed by five and a half years of one-weekend-a-month meetings and a two-week summer camp every summer for five years.

The Vietnam War was just heating up, and at the time the guard seemed to me the best option. I could fulfill my obligation and also receive real world business experience without going into combat. How hard could it be?

Little did I know that my decision to join the Army National Guard would put me right in the middle of one of the major Cold War conflicts of the century.

I was part of the massive force deployed for the Cuban missile crisis. This took place while I was on active duty, and so I was assigned to the first-on-the-ground strike force that was within one hour of landing in Cuba. We were to face some 50,000 Soviet troops who were already in Cuba. President Kennedy saved the day for everybody, including me, concluding negotiations just one hour before we were to be deployed. Talk about dodging a bullet. God the Father was there again for me.

There were also countless riot duty deployments for us in Chicago. The Guard proved to be a much bigger commitment than I had imagined.

GROWING UP

Looking back on my active duty in the army, I realize that all of those experiences were part of God's plan to help me grow up, physically, emotionally, and also spiritually. As a squad leader of a combat team, I learned how to give and to take orders, and I learned about responsibility and leadership, all things that were very necessary for the small-town boy from LaSalle, Illinois, to learn.

But the most important things that I learned and experienced had to do with spiritual maturity. That meant doing the right thing even when no one was looking. You can imagine the kind of test that was. Picture us: young soldiers get a weekend pass and go to town for fun and excitement. That meant heavy drinking (something I remembered well from my past life) and lots of available young women who hung out around army posts, looking for a good time with the soldier boys.

The military was an experience of both positives and negatives for me. On the one hand, it summoned and reinforced many positive things I had learned from my sister and her husband, values such as discipline and teamwork, which would end up being extremely important to my career and the business that I would later begin. At the same time, though, it was in the military that I got into the habit of blowing off steam in the same unhealthy way some of my buddies did, and I started drinking again—not to excess, and not as bad as my teenage gang days, but in a way that always seemed to lead to trouble and temptation.

It really is true: you become like the people you spend time with, and through the time I spent in the military, I found myself back off track.

Especially here, God the Father was present in my life. I won't go into the details, but in at least three situations while on weekend passes. In strange and mysterious ways he kept me from making seriously poor moral decisions, decisions that I would have regretted all my life. You can read between the lines on this one...God was there with me again, this time telling me, "This is not your place," reminding me of his plans for me in the future, and that I needed to stay pure in mind, body, and spirit.

OUT OF ACTIVE DUTY, INTO A NEW SALES JOB

It was August 1963. For the past eight months or so, I had been working for a Christian-owned firm in my first sales job at the age of twenty-one. The company was just entering the office furniture business after years of selling storage products to businesses around the Chicago area.

I had enjoyed surprising results in this, my first year in sales work. I found the job that I was made for. Everything was clicking for me professionally. I had found my niche: sales and design and furnishings that would improve the office workplace. Life was good. But I had been working hard, and I felt I needed a break.

THE ROAD TRIP

As luck would have it, I was invited to take a four-day driving trip with two friends, one of whom we would drop off at the University of Buffalo. We would drive up together and have some fun along the way. It sounded good to me. It promised to be a good time, with a stop in Pittsburgh to visit some school friends, drop off our friend in Buffalo, and make a stop in Ohio on the way home at a large theme park, which included wild rides and lots of young people and parties. My two friends and I had plans to have some major fun on this trip.

One of my buddies had arranged for us to stay overnight at a doctor's home near Pittsburgh. It was a long drive, and we had to stop along the way, so we found ourselves at this doctor's place. He was a fine man, he had a big family, and he had a big house. He was unfailingly polite to the three of us and gave us free lodging for the night.

Over dinner, he started talking about religion. My buddies and I looked at each other. We could hardly believe it—part of the price for staying the night and for the great dinner we were enjoying was listening to a sermon.

He went on and on, and his wife and daughters listened attentively. My buddies pretended to. I pretended to, as well, but then...

SOMETHING HAPPENED

Somehow I found myself getting caught up in what the doctor was saying. That voice in my heart said, "This is for you."

I can't remember exactly what he said, but I remember it began with him reading from the Bible. I'd been around churches for several years now, and I'd heard a lot of people talk about the gospel, but I can tell you that this was the first time that I'd actually received the gospel as something other than a social obligation.

This was odd, because there was no reason in the world for me to be listening so closely to what he was saying. The entire purpose of our stay there was contrary to anything the Bible had to say about how I should behave myself and how I should live my life.

Up to that point I had heard a lot of sermons, but I had never really listened to the gospel. Now I was listening as he spoke about Christ dying on the cross and paying for our sins and faith and the possibility of eternal life. I was spellbound.

I couldn't show that while my buddies were looking, though. So whenever I saw one of them glance at me from across the table, I had to do what they were doing, which was to stare down at the mashed potatoes on the plate. All the time, though, I was listening. And I was thinking about that moment in the dark, beneath the bridge, when I heard the words take my hand.

At one point in his little sermon, the doctor looked me in the eyes— not threateningly, but as someone who wanted to help. Someone who knew what I was up against. Someone who didn't want me going down the wrong path. I will never forget that look of his.

When dinner was over, my two buddies cornered me and told me that they wanted to head out that night. They didn't even want to spend the night. They weren't up for another sermon over breakfast. They had had enough sermons to last them for the rest of their lives.

I said I wanted to stay—I may have told them I was too tired to get back in the car again and drive through the night. The truth was, I wasn't ready yet to leave the feeling that had come over me at the dinner table. Reluctantly, they agreed to stay the night at the doctor's house.

We went to bed.

ON THE ROAD AGAIN

We got up early the next morning. There were no more sermons. We thanked the doctor. We hit the road.

That discussion at the dinner table stuck with me, though. It was like an arrow through my heart. I couldn't stop thinking about what the doctor had said, and how he had looked at me. I tried to shake it off. This was supposed to be a party trip.

After our stop at the University of Buffalo, we made our way as fast as we could to that big theme park in Ohio. I don't even remember the name of it. But somehow we met some girls there. We got involved and started talking about another overnight stop, this one a lot more fun than the one we'd been forced to endure at the doctor's house. The idea was to chip in for a motel room and show the girls a good time. We'd all been drinking, and my head was spinning. And I was saying all the things I was supposed to say about how great this night was going to be.

And then I saw the doctor's eyes again, just looking at me.

I realized I still had this arrow through my heart. I just couldn't do what we'd planned to do. I couldn't be a part of sharing a motel room with my friend and the women we'd just met.

I heard the voice say again: TAKE MY HAND.

CHANGING COURSE

My friend thought I was nuts when I told him I was going to sleep outside in the car.

I can only explain what happened to me as having the feeling that there was an angel sitting on my shoulder, just dragging me along, keeping me away from the wrong experience. I'm sure the others must have thought I had flipped out. But I didn't go into that motel. I slept out in the car. It was miserable, but I finally got a couple of hours of sleep.

The shortest, simplest, most honest, and most direct way to put this part of the story was that I had backslid...but after the night around the doctor's dinner table, I realized what I had done. I didn't have to backslide forever. I could be myself again. I could take the Father's hand again. And that's what I did.

The next morning, my friend and I made our way back home. It was a long and mostly quiet trip. I'm sure he thought I had suddenly gone nuts. But I was certain I was back on the right path.

Fast forward a week or so. I was going to my day job as a salesman, driving my little '61 Volkswagen down the street early in the morning, half asleep, trying to find something on the radio that would keep me awake.

As it happened, I stumbled across a religious station on the radio. It was one that I had never heard of before, called the Morning Chapel Hour. A man named Wilbur Nelson was the preacher. In the Chicago area, there's a bible institute called the Moody Bible Institute, and they have a radio station. That's what I landed on. I didn't know anything about it. It was just an accident—or was it?

So I was driving with my eyes half-open, overworked and under rested as usual. This guy Wilbur Nelson was talking about salvation, and all of a sudden he got my attention. He was talking about the gospel, the same thing that the doctor had been talking about at the dinner-table sermon. It was almost like it was the same conversation, just continued, and pouring through the car radio of my little Volkswagen bug. He even recited John 3:16, which was a verse that the doctor had shared with us in Pittsburgh.

For God so loved the world, that he gave his only begotten Son, that whosoever believeth in him should not perish, but have everlasting life.

I just couldn't believe how closely what he was saying matched up with what I had heard from the doctor, and with what I had been thinking about, on some level, ever since that night beneath the bridge. The chance for salvation. The role of the Savior. The opportunity for eternal life.

Then Wilbur Nelson reached a point in the sermon where he said, "If you're driving along in your car right now, and you heard the gospel just now, I want you to find a safe place to pull over by the side of the road. Just go ahead and do it. So pull over safely, and yes, I am talking to you.

And I thought, "Wow, how did he do that?" And sure enough, there was a spot waiting for me. I pulled the car right over. Of course I had to pull over. Of course he had been talking to me. I had heard the gospel.

I'd heard it just then, and I'd heard it at the doctor's house, and if I was really honest with myself, I'd heard it that night beneath the bridge. What else was I going to do but pull the car over?

I have often wondered how many other people who happened to be listening to that program that day pulled their cars over on the side of the road that day. I don't know what the real number was, but I know I was one of them.

And there, by the side of the road, Wilbur Nelson continued. It was like he and I were walking together, walking along the path the doctor had asked me to follow just a few days earlier. Over the radio, he said, "I want you to repeat this prayer after me." The voice in my head said, "Trust in me."

"OK."

He said, "I want you to say the words I say, OK?"

"OK."

He said, "I have made a mess of my life."

I said, "I have made a mess of my life."

He said, "I have gone my own way."

I said, "I have gone my own way."

He said, "I now consciously choose to welcome Jesus Christ into my life, to listen to him when he says 'Follow me,' and then to follow him."

He said, "Jesus, I want to trust you, and I want you to lead me and make me the kind of man that you want me to be."

I said, "Jesus, I want to trust you, and I want you to lead me and make me the kind of man that you want me to be."

He said "Amen," and I said, "Amen."

And from that moment on, I really was on the path. Everything in my life came together after that. I felt a peace that I had never felt before.

Who knew something like that could happen to you while you were headed down the road? The road I had been driving on had looked like any other road, but it turned out to lead to the road of my life's true purpose.

That was a powerful, impossible-to-ignore experience I'd had in that little VW Bug of mine. It changed my life. Or maybe the better way to put it would be to say that it gave me back my life.

For as long as I lived, I would never forget the sermon that I heard over the radio, never forget my decision to pull over by the side of the road and pray, never forget the feeling of rightness in my heart that had followed that prayer. It was one of those aha experiences. It really marked a coming of age for me.

Interestingly, I was twenty-one at the time, and so looking back, I think of it as the point at which I left my childhood behind and moved into adulthood. It was an experience of transformation. It was God speaking to me again.

After that experience, everything in my life started to change for the better again. The fabric of my life, which had unraveled a little during my time in the military, was assembling itself all over again, with a new, stronger thread. I could tell that it was somehow the same as the one that had held me back from disaster on so many dark events of my past life.

There is another thread—a thread of belonging, and purpose. My sister Rose and her husband had a very similar experience to the one that I had, and at just about the same time.

They, too, encountered the gospel message in a new and powerful way, and they, too, recommitted their lives to Christ. This was remarkable, because we were Presbyterians, and Presbyterians normally didn't go in for that kind of "revival" moment. Theirs and mine had been, almost exclusively, social gospel experience. It wasn't about these dramatic personal moments of recommitment. But now, within about a week of each other, and operating on two totally different tracks, we had all three recommitted ourselves to our faith. That was pretty remarkable, and it brought us closer together. Our faith united us in a powerful way. Our values were suddenly very clear, to ourselves and to each other. We were like three new people who had been brought together on a mission. And I felt the importance of that mission in a very powerful way.

All of a sudden I wanted to tell everybody what I had experienced. I kept getting signs that this was what I was supposed to do with my life. It was quite an interesting time.

SOME MONTHS LATER.

There came another day when I was driving down the highway. This wasn't the little VW. I had moved up in the world, and I was driving a nice sedan, with the engine in front and everything. I was becoming a very successful salesperson and enjoying every minute of it. Then I heard the voice again. This time it said, "Share your faith."

I was praying as I was driving, (I did that a lot since the radio sermon experience.) and I said, right out loud, "You know, you keep telling me, Lord, that I'm supposed to be sharing my faith with other people, and helping them find you, too. So, here I am. I'm on the tollway here in Chicago, and I'm on my way to a meeting. But that meeting is not as important as my responsibility to you. So if you want me to share the message with somebody right now, I will. Just make it happen."

I'm not quite sure what came over me to pray for that, but that's what I prayed for. Almost as an afterthought, perhaps to convince myself that what I had just said was a joke, I said, "Why don't you just bring someone to me right now?"

And at that very moment, there was a big puff of steam or smoke under my hood. I pulled over and saw that I had blown a radiator hose. I guess that was proof that even God has a sense of humor.

WHAT NOW?

So there I am, on the shoulder of the expressway, wondering whether that's really what is supposed to happen when you pray for a sign, and a guy pulls in right behind me. He gets out of his truck and says, "Hey, can I help you, buddy?"

I said, "Well, I just blew the radiator hose, and now I'm totally stranded. I would be very much obliged to you if you could give me a lift."

He said, "Come on, hop in, and I'll get you where you need to go. There's a gas station at the next exit."

Relieved, I agreed, and I got into his truck. Then I started thinking. Was there a purpose to all of this?

"Okay," I thought to myself, "is this the guy I'm supposed to say something to?" It certainly seemed like what I was supposed to do, but

I really felt out of my league. Then I thought, "Well, what's the worst that could happen?"

Before I could talk myself out of it, I started sharing my faith with him. I can't recall exactly what I said to him now, but I remember it involved telling him about my own life experiences, and about the prayer that I had made to God just a few minutes earlier. And I went on for about twenty minutes or so. I could tell he was driving in order to get me to keep talking, because we kept passing that gas station he had been talking about.

There came a spot where I stopped talking, and I was more than a little curious to hear how we would respond. What was he going to do? Kick me out of the truck?

And then the most amazing thing happened. He said, "You know what? That's what I want. That's what my life needs." And he took a deep breath and looked at me as though I had just given him a big hug. Which I guess, in a way, I had.

He started sharing his own story, which was pretty interesting, full of all kinds of challenges and choices and chances that seemed very similar to mine. Long story short, he had been thinking his life over in just the same way I had been thinking mine over just a short time ago.

Within a very few minutes, we were sharing all kinds of experiences with each other. It seemed like we had known each other forever. I shared the gospel with him, and he accepted Christ in his heart right then and there. And we exchanged phone numbers, and then we finally stopped at the gas station, and I got my radiator hose fixed and was back on the road again, and this time I knew just exactly where I was going in my life.

From that day forward, a big part of my life was all about sharing the gospel.

FELLOWSHIP

That experience with the man who gave me a ride was transformative. It was as if I had been given a red cape and a license to fly. Once it was clear to me that it was actually easy for me to talk to people about what had happened to me, I was okay with sharing it with lots and lots of people. I began to get more involved, not only in helping other people to experience what I experienced, but in helping members of my church to get better at reaching out to people to talk about the gospel without offending them or intimidating them. It turned out I was pretty good at that, too. So I began to teach that to others.

During this time, I shared the gospel with my mother and father, and with some of my siblings, too. Some years later, I founded the Chicagoland Evangelism Explosion Fellowship, which helped churches and individuals to share the gospel on a personal basis. And it had all started with a prayer I'd said while I was headed down the road—the road of life. In answer to that prayer, God told me to "tell others."

THE ROAD OF LIFE

At first, I saw God as my observer,

my judge,

keeping track of the things I did wrong

so as to know whether I merited heaven

or hell when I die.

He was out there sort of like a president.

I recognized his picture when I saw it,

But I really didn't know him.

But later on

when I met Christ,

it seemed as though life was rather like a bike ride,

but it was a tandem bike,

and I noticed that Christ

was in the back helping me pedal.

I don't know just when it was

that he suggested we change places,

but life has not been the same since.

When I had control,

I knew the way.

It was rather boring,

but predictable...

It was the shortest distance between two points.

But when he took the lead,

He knew delightful cuts,

up mountains,

and through rocky places

at breakneck speeds,

it was all I could do to hang on!

Even though it looked like madness,

He said, "Pedal!"

I was worried and was anxious

and asked,

"Where are you taking me?"

He laughed and didn't answer,

and I started to learn to trust.

I forgot my boring life

and entered into the adventure.

And when I'd say, "I'm scared,"

He'd lean back and touch my hand.

He took me to people with gifts that I needed,

gifts of healing,

acceptance

and joy.

They gave me gifts to take on my journey,

My Lord's and mine.

And we were off again.

He said, "Give the gifts away;

they're extra baggage, too much weight."

So I did,

to the people we met,

and I found that in giving I received,

and still our burden was light.

I did not trust him,

at first,

in control of my life.

I thought he'd wreck it;

but he knows bike secrets,

knows how to make it bend to take sharp corners,

knows how to jump to clear high rocks,

knows how to fly to shorten scary passages.

And I am learning to shut up

and pedal

in the strangest places,

and I'm beginning to enjoy the view

and the cool breeze on the face

with my delightful constant companion, Jesus Christ.

And when I'm sure I just can't do anymore,

He just smiles and says..."Pedal."

—Author Unknown

LOVE

The next part of my story jumps to how I met Carol, the woman who would eventually become my wife. She is a very special woman, gifted in more ways than I could possibly list here.

I met Carol in our church. She was attending a teacher's college in

Iowa, but she came home to visit with her parents from time to time and went to the church that her parents went to, and that I happened to go to as well. Once we started talking, we both felt this complete comfortable connection. It was almost like we were born to talk to each other.

Our first meeting was at a college bible study at the home of our pastor. I came in late, after work and my classes, in a three-piece suit that my dad would have been proud of. Mr. Button-Down.

I saw a pretty girl I thought I knew across the room and said, "Hi, Gail." (Gail was an old friend of mine.) Everybody laughed. It wasn't Gail, it was Carol! They did look similar. I was embarrassed.

She would say it was love at first sight.

The following Sunday, I saw Carol again at church. We had coffee and a long, very nice talk. This was the end of Christmas break, and Carol had to return to school. She was leaving that day to go back to college in Iowa, and we agreed to say in touch, which we did, by mail. We both knew something good was happening between us.

There were a few phone calls back and forth until Easter vacation and our first date, a movie, and coffee and ice cream after—followed by several dates over Easter break and then lots more phone calls and letters.

When school ended for the year, I asked Carol if I could pick her up at school and bring her back home. She agreed. We had more dates, and my main memory of those early times was that we always had something to talk about—a good sign. We just loved talking to each other, usually over coffee and ice cream. It was a magical summer.

THE STILL SMALL VOICE

This too was a case of God's hand guiding our lives. I clearly remember exactly when and where we were when God spoke to me again, in that still small voice in my heart. The voice said, "This is the woman that you should marry."

The two of us were in my car, returning from Sunday evening club worship service in downtown Chicago, at Orchestra Hall. I heard that voice, and I knew what I had to do. But it took me a little while to get my nerve up.

Shortly thereafter, when I got my nerve up, I asked Carol for her hand in marriage. She said yes—another blessing from God.

As I mentioned, she would tell you today that she fell in love with me on that very first night that we met, and that she knew I was the man she wanted to marry the moment I called her by the wrong name. I didn't get there quite as fast as Carol did, but before long I certainly knew I was interested in spending more time with this engaging, intelligent, beautiful, downright magnetic woman. The magical summer ended with our making plans to marry the following year in August.

And we did just that, on August 14, 1965. Just as an aside, on our wedding day, at the beginning of the ceremony, a cardinal flew in through the open window of the church, and sat on a ceiling beam for the entire service, and then flew right back out the window. Since that day, the cardinal has always been our favorite bird.

THE JOURNEY CONTINUES

After we were married, of course, we learned a lot about each other. It's like that in every good marriage. The moment you stop listening to each other, you are in trouble. We were doing fine, but we had the regular ups and downs during our first year of marriage. We both had new and very demanding jobs—Carol as an English teacher at a local junior high school, and me as a new, straight commission salesperson for an office furniture company.

Carol grew up in a traditional Presbyterian home and church environment and was always a good example of Presbyterian values and moral standards. Yet she had never made a personal profession of faith by asking Jesus into her heart and life for salvation. One day, during one of our more heated discussions, I suggested that just maybe she should take that step of faith and invite Jesus into her heart, asking him to lead her life.

She surprised me by saying, "I would love to do that."

We prayed together, and she invited the Lord into her heart! This was a huge event for both of us, because now we were unified in our faith together. It was like a whole new beginning for us as a couple. It happened on September 22, 1966.

MY FATHER AND I SHARE A CAR RIDE

My reconciliation with Dad took place years later. It started out from an unexpected point: my mom's decision to receive Christ.

Dad had seemed distant about this when he first heard about her choice. I had shared the gospel with my mom, and as a result of those discussions, she eventually came to embrace the same spiritual path that Carol and I and so many others had embraced. She was very receptive; he folded his arms and kept his distance. He listened, but he didn't take any action for several years.

Until my mom got sick.

She was in the hospital, dealing with a heart condition, and struggling. And I think my dad had to come to terms with the possibility that, given the seriousness of her situation, he might just be alone before too long. That reality changed him. It sobered him.

After a long spell of sitting together in the waiting room, and eventually getting some time with my mom, my dad and I made our way out to my car. During the drive home, we talked about his faith, and the fact that he had not made a step of faith a few years earlier, when my mom had. I reminded him about his favorite wooden sign in the tailor shop, the one that read: "Too soon we get old ... too late we get smart." I asked him whether he would reconsider his choice, and do what Mom had done: accept Christ and have the security of knowing that there was a home waiting for him, a heavenly home, if he were to die. He began weeping quietly.

During that ride home, he prayed with me, and he asked God the Father to come into his life. The big distance between us had vanished. We were both home again.

ANSWERED PRAYERS

Later in our marriage, our daughter, Lisa, and our son, Paul, at about five or six years old, asked Jesus into their lives as well. Married life is truly an exciting Spirit-filled work in progress, filled with answered prayers of praying parents. And now, forty-eight years later, Carol and I still feel the hand of God The Father on our family, and we feel that our life together gets better every year.

TWO PIECES OF ADVICE FROM CHARLIE

I pray you have the blessing of a strong marriage. Charlie 'Tremendous' Jones, the author of a great book called The Price of Leadership, was once asked, "How have you managed to stay married to your wife Gloria for so long? What's your secret?" They had been together for many decades. His answer was simple enough. "She won't leave me!"

That short answer had a lot more wisdom to it than you might think. If you want to have a great marriage, don't leave. Be present. Show up and participate in the other person's emotional life. Don't walk away. Don't check out. Be there for your spouse. Don't leave, and you won't be left. That's how it has worked for me.

I pray you find your purpose in life, the purpose that God the Father has established for you. Charlie had another piece of wisdom that I felt I just had to share with you. Like his advice on marriage, it seems obvious enough the first time you hear it, but it is worth studying closely. Charlie wrote, *"Things don't go wrong and break your heart so you can become bitter and give up. They happen to break you down and build you up so you can be all that you were intended to be."*

In a good marriage, and in a good life, we encounter obstacles as we journey through time. That's just what happens. If you believe these obstacles present themselves for a reason, if you believe that the reason connects to the plan that God the Father has for you, then you and I are brothers, and God is our Father. I hope this book has been helpful to you, and I hope your journey takes you home.

FATHER'S DAY

Today is Father's Day, 2013. I'm holding the pipe that my dad used to smoke. The rich tobacco smell from the pipe transports me back to my childhood days, and I remember hiding out in my dad's tailor shop, watching and listening to him work. I clearly remember the father-and-son times we shared as we sat together around the huge Philco radio on Sunday nights, listening and learning about the great stories from the Bible. And I remember working, and sweating, and getting my hands dirty in the soil of Northside, his amazing garden, where we boys learned to enjoy good work.

Finally, my eyes fall upon the wooden sign that hung for so many years in my father's tailor shop, and now hangs in my study. It was his favorite saying: "Too soon we get old...too late we get smart."

Funny, isn't it, how much pleasure we derive from the simple memories of childhood. Each one of them is precious. Today, Father's Day, I'm still so very proud, so very happy, to be the tailor's son. Thank you, Dad.

EPILOGUE

That's my story of my search for the Fatherhood of God: a teaching parable that I'm proud to dedicate to my father, John Klobucher. I hope that now that you've read it, you will pass it along to someone who will benefit from it.

And if you are also one of the millions of men who are still seeking the love and closeness of the father you never had...I hope you will open the door of your heart to the Father God, and allow him to fill the hole in your heart where your father should have been.

Behold, I stand at the doorway (of your heart) and knock.
If anyone hears my voice and opens the door, I will come
into him, and I will dwell there. Revelations 3:20

"Who is your father? Who is your father? Oh, wait, I know you—you are God's son! I see the resemblance. You are God's son. This is your family, you are always welcome here!"

Appendix A

Why Fatherhood Is So Important To Children

The father factor: Data on the consequence of father absence
According to the US Census Bureau, twenty-four million American children—one out of three—live in biological-father-absent homes. This amounts to a vast shadow, a "father factor" that looms over most of the social issues facing America today.

The negative effects of father absence plays a statistical role in all of the following national challenges:

- poverty

- infant health problems

- incarceration

- crime

- teen pregnancy

- child abuse

- alcohol abuse

- drug abuse

- childhood obesity

- underachievement in education

What can you do to make the numbers look better? Read on.

APPENDIX B

The Father Guide

Twelve steps to help you become the father that every son wants and needs.

Here is an unscientific list of ideal father to son characteristics.

See how many you might have missed out on...and how many you might be able to share with the son in your life. Note: This is not meant to be a complete list. Feel free to add a few items of your own!

I should also add that I can't claim to have been an expert in all the steps to good fathering myself. I, too, am a work in progress when it comes to being a good father (and grandfather). By God's grace, we will never stop learning to become the fathers that we were meant to be.

1. **"Do what I say *or* what I do!"** A son's eyes are always on his father, and he will always do what you do, regardless of what you say. So try to be a great role model. Remember: Fathering is listening, loving, learning, teaching, and sharing. Try to set a good example by being a good listener, especially when it comes to your son. Children will tell you what is wrong, as long as you're willing to listen to them. An emotionally healthy son needs to be communicated with often.

2. **Teach and learn together.** Tell stories that have a learning message. Seek out great stories of faith and share important lessons that you and others have learned. Tell and read stories to your son. Pick stories that mean a lot to you personally. Your son will remember them all of his life.

3. **When you fail (and you will), admit it and correct it.** Use that experience as a teaching moment for you both. Ask for forgiveness sooner rather than later. Acknowledge your own vulnerability to failure, to sinfulness, and to making poor choices. Warn of the evil and temptations that surround us all.

4. **Be a spiritual model for your son.** Be a praying dad. (See The Father's Prayer For His Family. Page 147, Appendix C) Pray for your son and all of your family members. Pray together at

mealtimes and at bedtimes. Pray for God's protection of your family. Pray for your children's spouses, even the unknown "to-be-spouses," in the case of younger children. Celebrate together all the answered prayers, and celebrate, too, God's leading role in your lives.

5. **Be a happy father.** Have fun, and remember that even being silly is okay. Play together. When you play sports, make sure you don't win too often. Learn to laugh. Watch that joy in your son's eyes as he experiences your huge belly laugh. Have a joyful spirit!

6. **Work together.** This can happen on or off your "day job." Take every opportunity to get your hands dirty together and share a job. Let your son help. Demonstrate that work is fun and good. Find projects that will help others. And don't forget to bestow a treat or a nice surprise after a job well done.

7. **Help your son to develop manly ways.** Be gentle, but firm; be kind and slow to anger. Take pride in your own work. Show up on time. Do what you say. Always finish what you start. Say please and thank you. Set boundaries; practice discipline and self-control. Show love and respect to your wife, your mother, and to all girls and women. Practice a good handshake and make good eye contact while shaking that hand. Model the

conversational style of listening and talking. Answer questions with full sentences. Teach all these things, practice them, point out good examples of them, and compliment your son's successes in these areas, even if they are small.

8. **Be positive.** Don't be critical and negative. Avoid excessive criticisms. Forgive and forget. Don't compare your son to others. Extend open arms and be accepting. Spend time together. Encourage conversation and accept all questions. To the degree that you can, be available to talk whenever your son is ready to talk. When there is a problem, focus on the problem, not on the son.

9. **Remember that a son seeks approval and wants to please his father.** Encourage and compliment your son. Help him find ways to please you. Find good jobs for him to do, jobs that he can be good at, and then show your pleasure at his effort. This will brighten his spirit more than you'll ever know.

10. **Show your son a big, loving heart.** Practice showing affection and father/son love. Demonstrate camaraderie, protection, and strength. What you say and how you act toward your son will be how you will be remembered. Always strive to be your best vision of yourself in the eyes of your son, and he will bless you for it.

11. **Coach, teach, and discipline with love.** Strike a balance between leniency and firmness. Point your son toward other people who can help with learning, like a grandfather, uncle, teacher, pastor, coach, youth leader, or any other good male models.

12. **Show your son how much you value him each and every day.** Your son's lifetime sense of self-worth, and his respect for others and his God, will be shaped by the way that you value him. Let him know he is precious to you!

Appendix C

Afterword (The Father's Legacy)

The father's prayer for his family.

Early on in our married life, my wife Carol and I found ourselves deeply moved by the ministry of Mark Bubeck, our pastor, at Judson Baptist Church in Oak Park, Illinois. This godly man led us as a young couple to focus on the Scriptures, on prayer, and on evangelism. I was most inspired by his strong emphasis on being a praying father. He wanted fathers to leave a legacy of a prayerful life for their families, and this became a primary focus of mine. On occasion, I watched our pastor model that value of prayer in his own family.

This constant focus on prayer led to Mark's book *Raising Lambs Among Wolves*, in which our family had a small cameo role. The book shows parents how to protect their children through prayer and helps lead them into a life of spiritual victory, fulfillment, and freedom.

I'm proud to include an excerpt from the book, with Mark Bubeck's permission. I should tell you a few things about this story, which features our family. Both our daughter, Lisa, and her brother, Paul, were attending Wheaton College at the time it was written. Lisa was a junior then, and Paul a freshman. While they were younger and still at home, I had made it a habit of praying for them, just inside their bedroom doors, as they slept in their rooms.

FOOTPRINTS IN THE CARPET

While home from college for a weekend break, Lisa came quietly into the kitchen, where her mother was busily preparing dinner. A vivacious junior in college, Lisa seemed pensive, as if spiritually moved. Her bouncy zip was subdued, her mood sober. Emotions were near the surface; in fact, as she spoke, her eyes were brimming with tears.

"Mom, is Dad still going into our room every night, like he did before we went to college, to pray for Paul and me?"

Carol was not prepared for the question. She knew Tom was dedicated to his long-standing, intercessory prayer vigils for their children, and she respected his dedication and heart. The prayers were a very private and sincere matter with her husband. Now she wondered how to respond to her daughter's question. Her daughter's directness seemed to necessitate a straightforward response

"Yes, he is," Carol answered, "but how did you know?"

"I saw his footprints in the carpet," Lisa replied. "I never knew that would mean so much to me!"

The tears were coming more freely now. "I guess I'm growing up, and my value system is different."

Lisa's response to her father's prayers should be noted here. Her tears of appreciation show us how parents can leave "footprints" in their children's lives, footprints of prayer, children often follow. Footprints that can lead them away from evil and along the path of safety.

That's the end of the excerpt. As this book goes to press, Lisa has completed her college degree, is married, and is busy raising three beautiful children with her Christian husband, Mark. Our son, Paul, who also graduated from Wheaton College, is married to his lovely wife, Amy, and has two children. Paul is the successor president of our thirty-five-year-old family business and is assisted by our son-in-law, Mark, who is a senior manager in the firm. We all live in the same town, and we worship and serve in the same church family. My dear wife, Carol and I are still praying for our family of eleven. And, there are still lots of footprints in the carpet!

God does answer prayer.

Tom Klobucher

My mom and dad's wedding picture taken in 1927 in Cadillac, Michigan.

My dad, John Klobucher, next to his 1922 Chevy
on the trip home to LaSalle, Illinois

My mother, Rose Ann Klobucher, in dad's 1922 Chevy on the way
home to LaSalle, from Cannonsburg, PA and their honeymoon

Dad's tailor shop in LaSalle, Illinois

The Tailor in his shop

The Tailor in his shop

Tom as a baby

Tom at 2-years old

Tom at about 7-years old

Our family of 7 - Tom in middle

Tom at 15 - The Rebel years -- Trouble ahead.

Tom and my sister Rose's family in the Chicago Area

I'm in the army now

Carol and Tom Klobucher, newlyweds, four months after we
were married in Bellwood, Illinois on August 14, 1965

Our family of four in 1974

Tom with Mom and Dad Klobucher

Our tribe of eleven in 2012

Tom and Carol Today, 2013

Tom Klobucher

Thomas Interior Systems, Inc.

476 Brighton Drive

Bloomingdale, Illinois 60108

630 980 4200

www.thetailorsson.com

www.thegreatworkplacerevolution.com

www.thegreatworkplacetransformation.com

www.thomasinterior.com